"Everyone who reads this book with understanding and acceptance of its truths will be transformed into a victorious Christian. This is a book that every Christian needs to read. Jesus said that when we know the truth it will make us free. The truths found within this book will set the reader free to live a victorious Christian life and fulfill his or her destiny."

—from the foreword by **Dr. Bill Hamon**,
bishop, Christian International Apostolic Network (CIAN);
author, *The Day of the Saints* and eight other
major prophetic and apostolic books

"A book on Jezebel needed to be written. Not only has Sandie done so, but she included two other women, Athaliah and Delilah. Sandie has keen insight into this realm, as well as strategies for dealing with the threefold cord. This book will help pastors, leaders and saints who long to move into the fullness of the destiny and inheritance. I highly recommend this book."

—**Barbara Yoder**, senior pastor, Shekinah Christian Church;
apostolic leader, Breakthrough Apostolic Ministries Network

"Believers often struggle with unseen forces designed to defeat them in their God-given destiny. Sandie Freed exposes three of these demonic spirits that frequently hinder the Lord's people. Practical steps to victory are included in this masterpiece that will help believers defeat the networking of the spirits of Jezebel, Athaliah and Delilah. I highly recommend this book for all who want to live the victorious life promised by Jesus!"

—**Barbara Wentroble**, founder, International Breakthrough
Ministries; author, *Prophetic Intercession, Praying with Authority,
You Are Anointed* and *Rise to Your Destiny, Woman of God*

"Wow! Sandie's new book, *Breaking the Threefold Demonic Cord*, blew my socks off. It's a cornucopia of little-understood biblical terms, their true meanings and how they relate spiritually to the 'lockdown' of our lives and destinies in devouring dungeons. I could preach a Disneyland of messages from this book!

"Because manipulative Jezebel spirits have invaded and torn gaping holes in my life and ministry in the past, it is a cold cup of living water to receive Sandie's revelations on how the seductive and religious spirits of Jezebel, Athaliah and Delilah work together as a threefold cord. They compromise, discourage and enslave us through false prophecies, witchcraft and fleshly enticements.

"This book not only opened my eyes to how these diabolical spirits attack and devour our destinies, but it gives awesome scriptural principles and prayers for casting down their strongholds for eternity. This book is a roller-coaster ride to freedom!"

—**Dr. Gary L. Greenwald**, apostle, Eagle's Nest Ministries

BREAKING *the* THREEFOLD DEMONIC CORD

How to Discern and Defeat the Lies of Jezebel, Athaliah and Delilah

SANDIE FREED

Chosen
Grand Rapids, Michigan

Published by Chosen Books
A division of Baker Publishing Group
P.O. Box 6287, Grand Rapids, MI 49516-6287
www.chosenbooks.com

Fourth printing, September 2008

Printed in the United States of America.

Library of Congress Cataloging-in-Publication Data
Freed, Sandie, 1951–
    Breaking the threefold demonic cord : how to discern and defeat the lies of Jezebel, Athaliah, and Delilah / Sandie Freed.
        p.   cm.
    ISBN 978-0-8007-9436-1 (pbk.)
    1. Spiritual warfare. 2. Satan. 3. Jezebel, Queen, consort of Ahab, King of Israel. 4. Athaliah, Queen of Judah. 5. Delilah (Biblical figure) I. Title.
BV4509.5.F7465 2007
235'.4—dc22   2007032499

All Hebrew and Greek translations are taken from the *Enhanced Strong's Lexicon* (Oak Harbor, Wash.: Logos Research Systems, Inc., 1995).

All English word definitions are taken from *Noah Webster's First Edition of an American Dictionary of the English Language* (Chesapeake, Va.: Foundation for American Christian Education, 2005).

All meanings of biblical names are taken from Judson Cornwall and Stelman Smith, *The Exhaustive Dictionary of Bible Names* (Gainesville, Fla.: Bridge-Logos Publishers, 1998) and Walter A. Elwell, *Baker Encyclopedia of the Bible* (Grand Rapids: Baker, 1997).

I dedicate this book to those who press daily in the pilgrimage to hear and touch heaven so that revelation and understanding may change the world. If you seek answers you will find them, and as you knock, the door of revelation will be opened. God's strength will empower you to make each difficult place a River of Life.

> Blessed is the man whose strength is in You,
> Whose heart is set on pilgrimage.
> As they pass through the Valley of Baca,
> They make it a spring;
> The rain also covers it with pools.
> They go from strength to strength;
> Each one appears before God in Zion.
>
> Psalm 84:5–7

Contents

Acknowledgments   9
Foreword   11
Introduction   13

1. The Threefold Demonic Cord   17
2. Jezebel's Evil Influence   39
3. The Gods of Jezebel   67
4. Confronting Jezebel   85
5. Athaliah's Reign of Terror   99
6. Praying against the Demonic Powers of Jezebel and
   Athaliah   121
7. The Evil Power of Delilah   143
8. Praying against Delilah and Dagon   165

Conclusion: See and Believe!   181
Notes   187
Recommended Reading   189

ACKNOWLEDGMENTS

I have two sets of parents who have forever changed and influenced my life, my family and my ministry. First are my birth parents, Bud and Dena Davis, and second are Bishop Bill and Evelyn Hamon, my spiritual parents. Each of them has blessed and empowered me with life, courage and endurance.

To my husband, Mickey, my lifelong friend and companion of over thirty years, and to Kim and Matt: You continue to inspire me and give me space to touch heaven and then return. You have taught me to laugh, take time and realize how important it is to live each day to its fullest.

To our Zion Ministries family, my sister Pam and especially my personal intercessors: This book would have been impossible without your faithful support, prayers and spiritual warfare. Together we have heard heaven's voice and prophetically moved forward into greater destiny.

To my Christian International family: It is an honor and privilege to be among the company of apostles and prophets who remain committed to proclaiming truth and restoration to the Body of Christ.

To Martha Milting: You were my first spiritual mother. Your godly insight opened my eyes to understand the fullness of the Gospel. Thank you for introducing me to transformation.

To Jane Campbell and Grace Sarber: We have completed another project together by the grace of God. Thank you both for your encouragement and support as we labor together for the sake of His Kingdom.

FOREWORD

God has anointed Sandie Freed with the Spirit of wisdom and revelation. She has the same anointing as the sons of Issachar, who discerned what God's people should do to gain victory over their enemies.

Most theologians declare that everything that happened in the natural in the Old Testament is a type and shadow of what takes place spiritually in the New Testament Church. The book of Hebrews uses the tabernacle of Moses with all its furniture, functions, sacrifices and offerings to explain Jesus and His Church. The apostle Paul declared this to be a proper hermeneutical practice in Romans 15:4 and 1 Corinthians 10:6, 11.

In this book Sandie Freed follows this principle by taking three characters from the Old Testament—Jezebel, Athaliah and Delilah—to reveal many weapons the devil uses against God's people. Sandie not only reveals these evil attitudes, attributes and spirits, but she also shows us how to pray effectively against them and to powerfully overcome them.

Everyone who reads this book with understanding and acceptance of its truths will be transformed into a victorious Christian. This is a book that every Christian needs to read. Jesus said that when we know the truth it will make us free. The truths found within this book will set the reader free to live a victorious Christian life and fulfill his or her destiny.

Dr. Bill Hamon
Bishop, Christian International Apostolic Network (CIAN)
Author, *The Day of the Saints* and eight other
major prophetic and apostolic books

INTRODUCTION

"The book needs writing, and the devil needs exposing!"

What in the world am I doing? Who am I to believe I have the spiritual goods to write a book that discloses such powerful evil forces? Since the first day I penned my thoughts, I have encountered discouragement, depression and insecurity. I know I have cried out for Your mysteries to be revealed, but I did not know it would be this hard! And then, how do I share what You have revealed? How do I truly express the importance of overcoming the seductions of the enemy? Please let me go. I want to be released from this assignment! I do not want to write this book. Surely someone else could do a much better job on this subject!

Oops! Excuse me! I did not realize you were listening to my conversation with God. Allow me to fill you in a little more. It has been much more than an exchange of dialogue; it has been a wrestling match with the Lord. Like Jacob, the Old Testament patriarch, I wrestled with the Lord throughout the entire night until the break of day (see

Genesis 32:24–25). The Holy Spirit led Jacob into a place he did not want to go. He wanted out of his assignment, just as I wanted out of mine. Jacob held on to God until he received a blessing. I was holding out for mine.

The frustration that led to the conversation was the result of intense spiritual warfare. Satan hates exposure and was going to extreme measures to remain hidden. My mind was tormented with demonic thoughts of hopelessness, failure and complete inadequacy. I was buying into the devil's lies and had succumbed to his seductions by desiring never to complete this book you are now reading. The very subject on which I was writing—the seductions of the enemy—made a "U-turn" and came back to seduce me into breaking a vow I had made to the Lord: a vow of obedience. Yet this present challenge made me want to run away like Elijah and find a cave. For weeks I had suffered from insomnia due to nightmares. Each revelation was met by demonic resistance. I was physically drained from penning my thoughts. I questioned my purpose, my calling and my ability. On this particular night, I felt totally defeated in my futile attempts to expose another plan of the devil. I begged God to release me from the assignment.

When Jacob's wrestling match ended, God blessed him and changed his name from *Jacob*, "the supplanter," to *Israel*, "prince of God." When mine ended, I did not necessarily receive a name change, but I did receive an answer. The Lord said, *The book needs writing because the devil needs exposing.* That was it. No great blessing. No words such as, *Thank you so much for trying. You are off the hook. I will use someone else.*

But then another part of the answer came. I fell asleep and had a dream that empowered me with a fresh determination to rise up and fulfill my commission.

The Dream of Hell

I walked through a pitch-black corridor. *Where am I?* I was straining to see. Although I was holding a candle to light my path, I could barely see my hand in front of my face. Fearful I would bump into a wall, I held the light as far forward as I could. The walls seemed to be made of mud and filth, appearing so unclean that I determined to stay clear of them. It seemed I was making my way through an underground sewer, and the pathway was so twisted and narrow that I could barely get through.

Suddenly a most gruesome face darted past me. When the grotesque creature saw the light, it headed into greater darkness. The light seemed to torment this devilish being. Then I knew. *Oh, my Lord! I am in hell!*

I inched along even more slowly. *God, I don't really want to see another one of those.* . . . Two more totally horrifying faces sped by me, not wanting the light to touch them. I could hear them shivering in fear that I would shine light upon them. This was the end of my dream.

Demons Do Not Want to Be Exposed!

I jolted from the bed. I had seen hell for only a fleeting moment of time, and I can tell you this: I have no desire ever to go there again, even in another dream. Instantly I was aware that the Lord had answered my pleas. He had given me an important dream that revealed to me the evil forces that did not want to be exposed. I had been asking God if this book should be written, and now I was confident that this assignment was from the Lord.

15

The threefold cord is a hellish assignment of end-time seductions against the Church. He allowed me to see the threefold cord of seductive spirits and the filthy environment that defiles all that surrounds them. The dream revealed that these spirits thrive in uncleanness and darkness and cannot remain in any environment if approached by the Light. The spirits exposed in this book are being sent from the pit of hell to seduce God's children into sin and apostasy. I am now keenly aware that seducing spirits are terrified of exposure, and the Light of God's truth causes them to tremble in fear!

Many seducing spirits thrive in the dark places of our lives, and the Lord is exposing them. The gravity of this dream reveals that God is concerned for each of us, and He desires that we be freed from idolatry, curses of iniquity and generational strongholds.

My weapon against the devil and his plans of seduction is to expose him with the Truth and the Light! I have always enjoyed giving the devil the black eye. I have had to fight a lot of Goliaths in my day, and each battle proved victorious because God is faithful. Maybe this book is an extra "punch"!

So, here I go . . . continuing on my assignment from God because "the book needs writing, and the devil needs exposing!"

1

THE THREEFOLD DEMONIC CORD

And if one prevail against him, two shall withstand him; and a threefold cord is not quickly broken.

Ecclesiastes 4:12, KJV

"What was that?" The grating sound shook me to the core. I came to a complete halt as I attempted to locate the noise. It sounded like metal grinding against metal and a heavy latch being permanently fixed in place. I had the sense of being locked in a cage and confined. I immediately began to feel a sense of dread, hopelessness and despair. I glanced toward the television for an explanation of the sound, but it did not come from that direction. The noise continued to resonate within my mind, and I soon realized that I had heard something in the spiritual realm. Alarmed, I asked the Lord to identify the noise and its significance. Suddenly a sense of urgency overwhelmed me and I heard the words *demonic lockdown*!

I then recognized the sound. It was the clamoring that a vast number of prison doors makes as they slide across metal grids and lock prisoners into their cells. Though I do not fully understand the dynamics of prison confinement, I am aware that a prison lockdown is more than being confined for one night. The process involves an all-day confinement in which no one can enter or leave and all inmate movement is restricted. During lockdowns, no outsiders are allowed entrance—not even ministers of the Gospel! Any activity that alarms the prison system causes an immediate lockdown. The inmates are completely restricted until the lockdown is lifted.

I instantly became aware of Satan's plans to lock us into old patterns of destruction. God began to unfold revelation concerning a threefold cord of destruction that the enemy has planned against His Church to "lock it down." With this "lockdown," we are chained and imprisoned to the past with no hope of freedom. Satan's strategy is to imprison us and lock us into confinement that aborts our destiny and our increase.

We must realize, however, that if the enemy is planning a lockdown, then it must be our season to break out into an enlarged area. It is our destiny to be fruitful and to multiply! Look at what the Lord has planned for you:

"Sing, O childless woman! *Break forth* into loud and joyful song, O Jerusalem, even though you never gave birth to a child. For the woman who could bear no children now has more than all the other women," says the Lord. "*Enlarge your house*; build an addition; *spread out* your home! *For*

18

you will soon be bursting at the seams. Your descendants will take over other nations and live in their cities.

Isaiah 54:1–3, NLT, emphasis mine

Precious ones, did you hear what God has stated concerning your destiny? Notice the prophetic declaration He has made over your life:

- *Break forth.* God says you will break out of your old place and launch into the new.
- *Enlarge your house.* Get ready for something really awesome! God is adding a new room to your home.
- *Spread out.* Expect great expansion, and then extend your wings. You are getting ready to soar as an eagle and rise above negative situations!
- *Burst at the seams.* You are going to burst at the seams with joy! Those who have been "stuck" in the birth canal and feel they cannot come forth are going to be birthed into their destined places.

Dear reader, be certain of this one fact: It is your season to "break out" from old generational cycles that have confined you. Begin right now to anticipate your door to breakthrough opening wide. You are entering into your season of enlargement as the plans of the enemy are being exposed! Hallelujah!

The Lockdown of Hope Deferred

The enemy does not want you to experience freedom or to be birthed into your place of destiny. If Satan had his way, he would lock you down with "hope deferred." If you are like me, you have felt resistance as you have moved forward into your destiny. We experience the "press" as Satan applies pressure, attempting to lock us into old patterns of behavior and block every avenue of victory. If our hope of victory is thwarted, then we experience hope deferred.

Proverbs 13:12 states, "Hope deferred makes the heart sick." This means that when hope is prolonged, the heart is sickened and made weak. In the natural, a weak heart causes every organ in the body to suffer. If a heart muscle is not strengthened, the result can be death. It is the same in the spiritual realm. Unless our faith is strengthened, we will shut down. We must have the "heart" to move forward and be empowered with "heartfelt" tenacity to persevere. Yet when a strong demonic force opposes a breakthrough, it is increasingly wearisome to remain steady and consistent in spite of difficulties and discouragement.

The word *deferred* does not simply translate as "delay"; it also means that hope is "seized." The enemy is not simply planning to delay a promise; he desires to seize that promise! His desired result is death to promises, dreams and breakthroughs. If Satan can steal hope, then he can establish a "death structure" over a person's life.

Defining Death Structures and Strongholds

Because the enemy's ultimate desire is to cause death to lives and vision, we need to understand death structures. A *death structure* is created when the devil "builds upon" the past. In other words, past pain becomes a foundation upon which the enemy builds. Satan seeks to build upon past failures, disappointments and weaknesses. He then attempts to establish a strategy that becomes a "structure," resulting in death to vision and abortion of destiny. Once the structure is in place, he seeks to gain illegitimate authority over a life. If he has gained authority, then he can steal vision, hope and destiny.

I have always said, "If you ask the devil to dinner, he will bring his suitcase!" In other words, if you open any door, he moves in to stay! The devil advances into our lives to establish a stronghold. A stronghold does exactly what it states: it gets a hold on us that is strong. Jesus warned us of a "strong man" who desired to take our possessions (see Luke 11:21). A strong man has great strength and therefore has a "strong hold." The enemy will remain in a seated position of false authority until we overthrow and "dethrone" him. To dethrone Satan from his position requires that we operate in our God-given authority. Christ did not empower us to fight Satan with natural weapons but with supernatural weapons of warfare. To dethrone Satan's authority we are to "[cast] down arguments and every high thing that exalts itself against the knowledge of God, bringing every thought into captivity" (2 Corinthians 10:5).

Pulling Down Strongholds

A stronghold is any argument that sets itself up against the knowledge of God (see 2 Corinthians 10:5). It is a fortified place Satan builds to exalt himself. He attempts to possess our lives and appear bigger than God, and if he can do so, he gains a hold on us. Once we allow Satan to have a "seated" position, we have allowed him to be enthroned over us (see Revelation 2:13), and he must be pulled down.

21

A *stronghold* is translated as a "castle" or "fortress" and "anything on which one relies." Anything or anyone on which we rely can therefore become a stronghold over us. And like a strong fortress, the hold is so strong it is impregnable. This is a good thing only if we are relying fully on God and His Word. When we completely trust Him and believe His Word, then He becomes our high tower and our strength. But if we allow the enemy to seduce us and agree with his words, then he establishes himself as a stronghold and erects a death structure over us.

A stronghold is not pulled down through carnal methods. The apostle Paul instructed us not to fight with our natural understanding but to rely totally on God's Spirit as we battle against spiritual forces. We are encouraged to:

- cast down imaginations and every high thing that exalts itself against God;
- bring into captivity every thought;
- become obedient to God, His Word and His divine direction.

The Battleground Is between the Ears!

Let's examine the word *stronghold* a bit further. It is derived from the Greek word *echo*, and one of the meanings of *echo* is "to have possession of the mind and emotions." I have always believed that a stronghold involves Satan's hold on our minds and emotions, and this is the main stronghold we must overthrow! Any place in our lives where we have allowed Satan to reign can be considered a stronghold. Ephesians 4:27 says we are not to give the devil a place—meaning a foothold or position (in our minds, families, etc.).

22

Surrendering to emotions can hinder one's journey. Can you imagine how emotional it was for Abraham to leave his home and all that was familiar? Yet he was the patriarch of faith who followed the word of the Lord and remained steadfast and faithful. We must not despair or lose hope. As with Abraham, God will empower us to move beyond the emotions that attempt to hold us captive.

Paul encourages us not to be "conformed to this world, but [to] be transformed by the renewing of your mind" (Romans 12:2). To become transformed involves a process of change. *Transformation* is derived from the Greek word *metamorphoo* from which our English word *metamorphosis* is derived. Metamorphosis is the process a caterpillar endures as it is transformed into a beautiful butterfly. The entire process involves death to an old identity, experiencing a season of change and becoming an entirely new creation. This process is exactly what we believers experience as we are transformed into the image of Christ.

The enemy cannot have a hold on us if we renew our minds with His Word and perfect will. The process of renewing our minds involves three steps. First, we must be willing to change. Second, we are to present ourselves to the Lord as sacrifices in holiness. And finally, we must not be conformed, or fashioned, to this world. All three steps are dependent upon our becoming saturated with His Word. By daily "eating" His Word, our minds are fashioned and we come into agreement with His perfect will. As we implement what we learn, we can dethrone the enemy! And as we digest His Word, we gain knowledge and understanding of who we are in Christ Jesus. As a result, a new identity emerges, and we are therefore empowered to defeat every strategy of the enemy. We can rule and reign in this life through Christ Jesus (see Romans 5:17)!

Just a Word about Terminology

As strongholds are pulled down, we dethrone Satan from his seated position of authority. In Revelation 2:12–17 Jesus Christ rebuked the church in Pergamos for allowing Satan to have a throne there. Many in that place had allowed him to rule over them, thus giving him authority and a "seated position." I have always believed that when Jesus addressed the seven churches, He was talking to them as both a corporate entity and as individuals. Dethroning Satan is, therefore, an individual responsibility as well as the fruit of a corporate breakthrough. Once we dethrone the enemy from our personal lives, we can dethrone him from our families, churches, businesses and regions.

We have already observed the apostle Paul's instructions concerning our struggles against evil, consisting of specific levels of authority. In Ephesians 6:12 Paul writes, "Our struggle is not against flesh and blood . . . but against the powers of this dark world and against the spiritual forces of evil in the heavenly realms" (NIV). This translation uses the general terms *powers* and *spiritual forces of evil* to describe Satan's organizational structure. The King James Version is more specific in naming certain levels of authority:

> We wrestle not against flesh and blood, but against principalities, against powers, against the rulers of the darkness of this world, against spiritual wickedness in high places.

At this point, I must pause and lay two theological ground rules concerning the proper application and understanding of such words as *principalities, powers, demons, forces of evil* or *spiritual wickedness.* First, it is clear that although Scripture separates these forces, all have their origin in one main source—Satan himself, the originator of evil. Also known by such names as Lucifer, Beelzebub and the prince of this world, Satan has his very own governmental hierarchy, which is meant to oppose the authority of God. The Lord has His own supreme structure and governmental organization, as laid out in Colossians 1:15–16:

> He [Christ] is the image of the invisible God, the firstborn over all creation. For by Him all things were created that are in heaven and that are on earth, visible and invisible, whether thrones or dominions or principalities or powers. All things were created through Him and for Him.

Satan is not an original but will continue to *copycat* all that God establishes. He has his own structure of "organized crimes" set against God and His Church.

I believe you will agree with me on a second ground rule: that Satan's evil organization represents all that he is. He truly is *the* evil one! Although you might disagree with my terminology concerning *principalities, evil forces* or *powers,* I am asking in advance for grace because I am still growing in revelation. I do not wish to contradict or dispute the understanding of others; rather, I hope to apply revelation *in addition* to what has previously been revealed, in an easy-to-read and nonlegalistic text. My heart's intent is to empower each reader to dethrone the enemy in every area needed.

The devilish forces of which I am writing are not garden-variety demons but possibly principalities and territorial rulers that affect us adversely, both corporately and individually. We do not live in "normal" times. What we presently experience every day is what I would consider "subnormal." We cannot rely totally on previous revelation, therefore, but are more compelled to press for fresh insight and godly instruction.

When Jesus addressed the church of Thyatira, He rebuked them for tolerating Jezebel. He was not speaking about the Old Testament queen who had ruled Israel centuries earlier; she was already dead. I believe Jesus was referring to an evil influence with the same characteristics as the Jezebel who seduced Israel to worship idols. Jezebel was a murderer, an idolater and a seducer, and Jesus was addressing a demonic force operating in Thyatira, characterized by the same nature. I consider the Jezebel spirit a principality since it had found an entrance into an entire city and into the individuals who lived there.

When Jezebel finds an entrance into our personal lives, by contrast, we are basically dealing with one or more demons under the direction of Jezebel. During spiritual warfare on an individual basis, we might battle against control, manipulation, seductive thoughts, fear or anxiety—all symptoms of a Jezebel-type attack. But this evil power can also can take over large regions and territories and attempt to seduce God's people into apostasy and idolatry. (More on the characteristics of Jezebel and her idols later).

According to *Vine's Complete Expository Dictionary of Old and New Testament Words*, the word *principality* is from the Greek word *arche* and translates as "to begin, to be first, the origin, and having at the first spoken."[1] It further translates as "ruler or chief." One can easily conclude that a principality is a "ruler" over a territory or region. (Rulers rule over lands and territories just as kings have a kingdom.) The Greek word *arche,* interestingly, is linked with our English word *architect.* An architect is the first one who actually has the vision of something to build and then lays out a plan and blueprint to follow. Satan has his own delegated authorities—architects in the spiritual realm who first lay out the vision of destruction and then gather demons to implement their plans.

My husband and I have been in ministry for close to twenty years and have built custom homes for more than 25 years. In all our years of building, not one architect has ever shown up on our job site. There were others who built on the job, but the architect had laid out the vision and allowed others to fulfill it. This is what I believe Satan and his principalities do as his vision to destroy the Body of Christ is devised.

Although I believe Jezebel is a principality, we are often battling an individual demon—one with a Jezebel influence. Jezebel is a ruler spirit, and the demonic forces of Athaliah and Delilah team up with her to oppose us. Jezebel would, therefore, be in authority, with the demonic forces of Athaliah and Delilah co-laboring with her to carry out her strategy.

My terminology, however, may not always be stated thus, and to be honest, I do not believe there are many absolutes concerning the correct usage of names of evil powers. Scripture is not clear on much more than that there *is* a hierarchy.

It is my opinion that all three beings are powerful forces that gain strongholds over our minds and emotions, as well as over our families, businesses and churches. Whether we refer to them as *principalities, forces* or *spirits* is less relevant than that their power must be pulled down and Satan dethroned.

For the sake of this book, let's agree not to become sidetracked and debate certain terms or phrases used to explain Satan's hierarchy and power structure. Otherwise we have given legalism the upper hand.

Now, let's continue to discover how the evil powers animating three Old Testament women—Jezebel, Athaliah and Delilah—seduced God's chosen, and are still affecting us adversely today.

Threefold Cords

As we pull down strongholds and demonic powers, we need to be aware of the threefold cord the enemy uses against us. Let's first examine the dynamics of a threefold cord.

The use of a triple braided cord, or rope, dates back thousands of years. Though ropes have been made of many different materials throughout the years, the most common rope used for its steadfast strength has been the triple braided cord. Modern technology has improved texture and durability, but in most circumstances a triple braided cord is still known for its tremendous strength. A rope with only two strands is not nearly as strong as a rope with three. The multiplication factor in the strength increases tremendously by the addition of one more cord. The strength of only two cords is unpredictable, but adding an additional cord proves an almost invincible might.

The concept of a threefold cord takes on an entirely new dimension when considering it in the context of spiritual warfare. We must consider the use of the number three in our warfare against principalities and powers of darkness. Ecclesiastes 4:12 states, "Though one may be overpowered by another, two can withstand him. And a threefold cord is not quickly broken." In other words, if one person stands alone, he can be overpowered by another. Two can stand back-to-back and conquer. But when a third person joins the fight, the three have much greater power—a sort of supernatural synergy—and can overtake the oppressor, because a triple braided cord is not easily broken.

In my recent book, *Dream On: Unlocking Your Dreams and Visions*, I discuss the importance of numbers, and in particular, the number three:

> Certain numbers relate to God and His Kingdom, but there are also numbers that relate to the kingdom of darkness. The number three, for example, is a godly number and represents the divine Trinity: God the Father, God the Son and God the Holy Spirit. On the other hand, if one were to dream of three demons, the dream would be interpreted as a union of forces—a threefold demonic cord—that could be difficult to overpower.[2]

When we encounter a threefold demonic cord, we can be sure that three different demonic strongholds are working together to bring destruction to the Body of Christ. And their interaction gives them great strength.

The "Teamwork" of Jezebel, Athaliah and Delilah

Now that we understand how powerful a threefold cord can be, we can see why the devil commissions his demons to work in threes. Let's examine one team of three in particular.

The three strong, seducing demonic powers of Jezebel, Athaliah and Delilah work as a determined team to enslave God's people. When these three forces ally together, an evil resistance—a threefold cord—is established. As a result, this unholy trinity implements a spiritual lockdown that blocks and aborts expansion, breakthrough and freedom.

The primary purpose of this book is to expose the tactics of this threefold cord and to provide prayer strategies and godly direction to overthrow its power. All three spirits are seductive, they rob our strength and finances, and they lock us into religious structures that block our breakthroughs.

Let's now look briefly at each of these three seductive demonic forces.

Jezebel

Jezebel is known as the evil queen of Israel who murdered prophets and threatened the life of Elijah. She was an idol worshiper, murderer, thief and manipulator. She operated in illegitimate authority when she stole Naboth's vineyard and co-labored with the sons of Belial to seize Naboth's inheritance. The spirit of Jezebel inflicts poverty, infirmity, divination and a spirit of religion. Jezebel also brings confusion, fear and doubt into lives and circumstances. Though this evil power has no gender, the seductive methods of a prostitute are used to entice us into compromise in any area of our lives. Rather than slaying Jezebel as Jehu did, we are easily seduced into tolerating her spiritual seductions! The demonic principality of Jezebel will abort destiny if we do not pray and war against this seductive spirit. In this book we will expose the idols of

Jezebel, examine her strategies of destruction and learn specific prayers that defeat this destructive spirit and her cohorts.

Athaliah—The Seed of Jezebel

Athaliah was Ahab and Jezebel's daughter. She was more determined and vicious than her mother! Athaliah murdered all her male descendants to ensure her illegitimate authority to the throne.

The spirit of Athaliah destroys the generations and generational blessings. This spirit goes after generational inheritance with "double trouble." The demonic force of Athaliah releases a more intense attack of false prophecy, witchcraft and divination. She blocks breakthroughs with her evil, seductive words, causing us to doubt God's covenant and our promised destiny.

Many Christians have targeted Jezebel but have focused little prayer against her daughter. We will closely examine this evil power's maneuvers, how she operates today and how to overpower her with godly prayers and confessions.

Delilah

When it came to getting what she wanted, the biblical Delilah was another model of demonic determination and stealth. She seduced Samson and robbed his strength and destiny. It was a slow seduction, but it was still successful. Delilah tried three times to seduce Samson; on the fourth attempt he experienced the lockdown. Samson failed to defeat the evil influence because he entertained the seduction rather than destroying it. Samson was enjoying himself as Delilah moved in for the kill! As a result, his destiny was stolen.

The enemy sometimes does this same thing to us, wearing us down little by little through seducing strongholds. When we entertain a demonic power, we play around with it; that is, we enjoy it for a season. Though our ultimate intention may be to destroy it, we are weakened to the point that our strength is gone before we realize it.

God's Excellent Way

To gain victory over the threefold cord, we must first understand that Satan is not God. The devil has powers, but none is a match for our Lord. Satan has his threefold cord—but so does God! He is a threefold cord all by Himself—the Father, Son and Holy Spirit. The number three represents completion, and His threefold dimension is the completion of who He is. He is divine perfection.

God's threefold principle is consistent throughout the Bible. The Tabernacle, for example, consisted of three dimensions: the outer court, the inner court and the holy of holies. Other examples of the threefold principle are these:

- Jesus is the Way, the Truth and the Life
- The Three Feasts: Passover, Pentecost and the Feast of Tabernacles
- Faith, hope and love

(For more detailed information on the biblical principle of the threefold measure, I recommend Kelley Varner's book, *The More Excellent Ministry*.)

The many three-dimensional attributes of God's character, purposes and plans are also referred to as His "excellent way."

The word *excellent* is the Hebrew word meaning "triple." It also means "a threefold measure," "an officer of a third rank" and "weighty" things. God has His "excellent way" of defeating the devil and exposing the light in the midst of darkness.

> Have not I written to thee *excellent things* in counsels and knowledge, that I might make thee know the certainty of the words of truth; that thou mightest answer the words of truth to them that send unto thee?
>
> Proverbs 22:20–21, KJV, emphasis mine

The three courts of the Tabernacle are one example of this; they were a type and shadow of Christ, who through His blood provided the "more excellent way."

Knowing that one of the glory attributes of God is represented in the "eternal weight of His glory," it is important to realize that the threefold measure also ushers in the glory of God. Since God's purposes and plans are revealed in three dimensions, we must take a serious look at the threefold cord that the enemy uses to hinder us from being completed in His glory. Satan's influence through the demonic powers of Jezebel, Athaliah and Delilah attempts to seduce us from experiencing the full measure of God's glory. The purpose of the enemy is to seduce us with doubt, unbelief and disunity with the Father's plans.

The "more excellent way" is to remain in complete unity with the Father's heart and plan for our lives. The more excellent way is a journey of completion and experiencing His glory. God is a threefold cord of power and glory and encompasses all that heaven desires to release to us.

"Teaming Up" with God

The next thing one must do to gain victory over the threefold cord is to embrace revelation. Take every opportunity to cast out any stronghold that attempts to exalt itself over God's truth, and then "team up" with His perfect will for your life.

His "excellent way" is to agree with Him—to team up with His Word. If we "agree" with God, He promises to answer our petitions. To agree means that we walk together with Him in harmony with His divine purposes. As we pray His Word over our circumstances, we agree with what He has already said and established. When we agree with God, we become connected to His indestructible threefold team: the Father, Son and Holy Spirit. So even when we pray alone, we are part of a team, because God is a complete triune team within Himself.

But, oh! When we gather together as two or three in a corporate setting and agree, we can send thousands upon thousands of demons to flight (see Deuteronomy 32:30). At times, you might grab a few prayer partners and really give the devil a black eye!

Renouncing the Spirit of Religion

Even as you read this book, the threefold cord of Jezebel, Athaliah and Delilah attempts to challenge and lock you down with a spirit of religion. The third thing one must do to gain victory over the threefold cord is to renounce this power.

In my recent book, *Destiny Thieves—Defeat Seducing Spirits and Achieve Your Purpose in God*, I discuss the religious spirit and how it involves legalism, which "locks" us into old patterns and causes us to resist new revelation or change. Remember when John the Baptist began to speak about the "new"? His message challenged the religious thinking of the time and stirred up the pharisaical spirit, causing such a resistance that it eventually led to John's death. The spirit of religion is a death structure that moves in quickly and prevents us from entering into expansion, breakthrough and freedom.

Do not resist the wind of change! Though we are moving forth in unfamiliar territory, we must have the blind faith to move! Like Abraham, trusting God and all His covenant promises empowers us to move into the new place God has for us. Always remember that being on God's team empowers us to defeat every death structure over our lives.

Praying against the Occult Spirit

Finally, in order to gain victory over the threefold cord, we need to be aware that an occult spirit attempts to hide revelation. The occult operates through witchcraft, control and manipulation, which are characteristics of Jezebel and her cohorts, but the occult also operates through hiding revelation. We must use our spiritual discernment when gaining revelation or we might easily tap into the occult.

Revelation and the occult are closely related. The word *revelation* means to take something hidden and reveal it. It involves the revealing of the "secret things." On the other hand, the word *occult* means to hide revelation and to keep it a secret. Revelation is to "reveal," and the occult attempts to keep things "unrevealed." As we gain deeper revelation, Satan attempts to twist our understanding, and therefore we can easily open doors to the occult if we are not careful. Many times the enemy tries to move in "mysterious" ways, and some people feel this is always God. This is why so many Christians become what I refer to as "spooky spiritual." God is the revealer of mysteries, but He is not always mysterious.

Have you ever known anyone who experienced a physical illness and could not find the root cause? Even after extensive tests, the doctors scratched their heads and wondered what the cause of the illness was. In such instances, the demon attacking the body was determined to remain hidden. This is what I refer to as an occult spirit because the word *occult* means "hidden."

When we are dealing with root issues that affect our destinies, this same spirit is at work. We must bind this occult spirit and pray for exposure so that we are not locked down and are free to experience all God has for us.

Heading Off Demons at the Pass

As you read this book, occult spirits will probably cause confusion and attempt to convince you to stop reading. You may have to stop periodically, lay your hands upon your head and declare that you have the mind of Christ. These occult forces need to be exposed.

In order to head off such demonic powers at the pass, let's first recognize any areas of our lives where Satan has attacked, bind him and his demons from operating further and plead the blood of Jesus over our lives. Consider the following list of symptoms. Place a check beside every area Satan has attacked. (You will name these as you repeat the prayer of deliverance at the end of the chapter.)

____ Fear and doubt

____ Religious mindsets

____ Stubbornness

____ Fatigue

____ Lies and deceit

____ Family deaths; premature death

____ Loss of passion for God. (The enemy will pervert godly passion into ungodly passion.)

____ Loss of zeal. (The key to overcome this is to ask God to be jealous over you! He will move in quickly to empower you to realize your covenant relationship.)

____ Feelings of not measuring up to religious expectations, which result in performance

____ Unclean thoughts

____ Control and manipulation

____ Hopelessness and discouragement

____ Depression

____ Sickness and disease; infirmities

____ Sexual molestation and any form of seduction

____ Complicated religious lifestyles. (The enemy constantly attempts to seduce us into believing that receiving from God is hard or difficult. Always try to remember that it is not hard to receive from God; simply use childlike faith to receive. Breakthrough is not due to our efforts; it is due to our obedience and His grace.)

____ Patterns of lustful behavior

____ Perversion

Now I encourage you to pray the following prayer, lifting up to the Father all checked areas above:

Father, I come to You pleading the precious blood of Jesus and thanking You for the blood of Christ, which is my hedge of divine protection. Lord, You are going to lock down my enemies and destroy the territorial demons that attempt to steal our land. I ask You to station Your host of angels around me and my family.

I take authority over death, destruction and despair. I bind every evil influence—Jezebel, Athaliah and Delilah, the occult spirit and all demonic assignments planned by the devil. I take authority over all spirits of divination and occult strongholds that attempt to steal life and destiny.

I thank You for the wind of Your Spirit that releases the prayers of the saints and brings life to my potential and my future. Thank You, Lord, that I am breaking out on all sides and experiencing divine enlargement. I, like Jael, drive a tent peg into the enemy's plans!

I realize that the enemy has attacked me with [list the different ways Satan has attacked you, your family, business, ministry, etc.; use the list you checked above and name them one by one].

I am fully aware that You have given me all power and authority over the enemy. I believe this is my season to dethrone Satan from every area of my life!

In the mighty name of Jesus Christ, Amen!

2

JEZEBEL'S EVIL
INFLUENCE

Notwithstanding I have a few things against thee, because
thou sufferest that woman Jezebel, which calleth herself a
prophetess, to teach and to seduce my servants to commit
fornication, and to eat things sacrificed unto idols.

Revelation 2:20, KJV

The gentle breeze brushed Naboth's face as he walked
through his vineyard. *I used to run among the rows of grapes
when I was a child*, he thought. *I did not understand the
importance of this vineyard at that time. How careless I was
as a child whenever I would stumble and fall upon these precious
vines!* A slow smile formed as a faint memory of his

father's voice echoed through his mind. *"Son! Don't play in the vineyard! These vines are precious to us! The fruit of these vines determines our future!"*

The vineyard was Naboth's inheritance. Something valuable passed down through the generations. Over the years it had become a great source of family pride, for it was known as one of the choicest vineyards around. The notoriety of excellence had become the family's signature label and brought the highest prices at market. The wine from Naboth's vineyard provided pleasure from the monotonous diet of the Hebrews and had become an extensive item of trade.

Naboth paused to examine the hedge that protected his cherished inheritance. He carefully eyed every possible entrance for thieves and noted each area to be secured against intruders. He stopped and peered from different angles to be certain that every single row of his vineyard was well protected.

As he began his climb to the top of the watchtower, his foot slipped on one of the rungs. *Hmm, this step needs replacing. The wood is probably rotting. I need to secure that before harvest. I would not want anyone to slip and fall.* Finally, standing at the top of the tower, he took several minutes to enjoy the panoramic view of his field. *It is a spectacular vineyard,* Naboth thought. *My inheritance!*

"Hey, there!" Naboth's silent thoughts were interrupted by a voice in the distance. "Hey! You in that watchtower! I need to speak to you!" Naboth could not see who was calling, but he descended the steps to greet the person behind the intrusive voice.

Naboth drew closer. *Oh, great! It's Ahab again,* he thought and mustered up more courage for another confrontation.

Ahab had come the day before to examine Naboth's vineyard. When Naboth told him he was not interested in selling, Ahab insulted him, saying the land was only good enough for a vegetable garden! Naboth knew better. This was the finest soil around.

No matter how much he offers me, thought Naboth, *I will not sell him my vineyard! Why, that would be like Esau selling his birthright! I just won't do it!* Naboth was now clenching his fists as he gained more determination in his resistance. *Though the Law of Moses states that ancestral property is to remain in the family and not be sold, my love for the land goes deeper than any written law!*

Naboth was right on all counts. Jezreel was known for its fertile soil. Even the city's name meant "reproduction and fruitfulness" and "the Lord sows." God had truly blessed this land, and Naboth knew God had given him this vineyard as the family blessing. Naboth was also aware of the tragic loss that Esau had experienced when he sold his entire birthright for a bowl of soup. Because of Esau's carelessness in guarding his inheritance, the Lord considered Esau His enemy. And according to the Mosaic Law, all ancestral property was to remain as a family inheritance, never to be sold. Ahab was not expressing simply a selfish interest in the property; he was displaying an open defiance of God's laws.

Naboth became immediately affronted and defensive when he realized Ahab once again had intruded into his vineyard. Knowing Ahab had no right to trespass beyond the hedges, Naboth lifted his head boldly, looked the king straight in the eye and was ready to go "toe to toe" with Ahab. "Yes, King Ahab, do you wish to speak to me . . . again?"

Ahab stood with his arms folded. He was tapping his foot against the ground and biting his lower lip in frustration. "Naboth, as I said yesterday, I want to purchase this vineyard. It is perfect for what I need—a vegetable garden. Gardening is a hobby of mine, and this land is close to my residence. I will give you a better plot of land somewhere else." Ahab's voice grew more demanding. "You really need to think about this! I am willing to pay generously for this land."

Naboth struggled to hold back his emotions. Memories of his father and his love for the land brought tears to his eyes. *Oh, how he used to cherish the fruits of his labor,* Naboth reminisced. *And then there were the times when he spoke to me concerning the importance of my inheritance . . .*

Naboth held his head high and boldly responded to the king's offer. "King Ahab, this is my inheritance. This vineyard has been in my family for generations. This land belonged to my father and his father before him, and even his father before him! My fondest memories revolve around this vineyard. If I sold this land, I would be betraying my family and the Lord, who has chosen to bless me. I cannot and will not sell."

King Ahab could barely believe his ears. His emotions alternated between anger and grief. He would neither acknowledge Naboth's refusal with another offer nor cordially say good-bye. Rather, like a spoiled child he sulked, shrugged his shoulders and turned to leave. Refusing even to look at the vineyard one more time, he hung his head low and made his way home, mumbling with every step.

Naboth watched Ahab until he was out of view, making sure he did not return to the vineyard. He secured the entrance gate and left for home. With a deep sigh of relief, Naboth assured himself that the challenge to take his inheritance was over.

At home, Ahab's servants came to attend him. He motioned them away and headed to his bedroom. Going straight to bed, he ordered his personal attendants to leave, giving specific instructions that he was to receive no food at all. Ahab refused to allow anyone into the room and remained in bed, sullen and regretful because he was refused the vineyard of his choice. He was accustomed to getting his way and for several hours the refusal from Naboth tormented his ego.

The servants gathered outside Ahab's quarters, and Queen Jezebel overheard their whispering. "What's this?" she questioned. "Where's the king?"

Jezebel always spoke with a demanding, offensive tone toward the servants. Though at times she attempted to appear soft and feminine, her spirit was obtrusive and evil toward everyone she met. Her every action was controlling and demanding, and she always got her way.

The main servant spoke up. "Queen Jezebel, the king will not speak to anyone, and he has refused all meals. When he arrived, he went straight to his bedchamber."

Jezebel attempted to enter Ahab's room. "Our queen, we plead with you not to enter!" the servants warned. "He gave specific instructions that no one was to enter—not even you!"

"We'll just see about that!" Jezebel was her normal intrusive self. Opening the door, she questioned Ahab, "What in the world is wrong with you? The servants said you would not eat. What has upset you so?"

Ahab remained with his back toward his wife, refusing to acknowledge her presence. He was acting like a child who, when refused his way, whimpers and throws a temper tantrum. "I went to see Naboth, the Jezreelite, and told him I wanted to buy his vineyard. I even offered to purchase another vineyard in exchange for his, but he refused my offer. He said the vineyard was his inheritance and that he would not give me his vineyard."

Jezebel was furious. "Who is the king around here? I cannot believe you would stoop so low as to beg! Now get out of bed and eat! You can rest assured that I will get Naboth's vineyard for you! Do I have to do *everything* around here?"

The king rolled his eyes in a defiant fashion and sighed. Sarcastically he murmured to his wife, "Even if you try, it is against the Mosaic Law. No Hebrew who honors his God will give up his inheritance. It is not even a matter of money to them; it is some kind of land thing. It's no use. Just go and leave me be!"

Jezebel, always determined to gain control and have her way, rushed to her desk to grab a writing tablet and pen. Her thoughts ran amok as she sought some type of strategy to acquire this property for her husband. *It is not the land I am interested in*, she thought. *It is the principle of the thing. No Hebrew is going to tell us what we can and cannot have! These Hebrews really underestimate my power!*

Jezebel pulled the chair up to her desk. She sat for a while scheming and devising a takeover strategy. After a while Jezebel concluded that not only would they acquire the property, but also Naboth would be punished for his arrogance. *How dare he think he can do this to us? Just who does he think he is?* Jezebel's thoughts had turned to revenge.

Hmm, my first step is to gain a following. Somehow I have to get the magistrates to obey my command. Let me see. . . . I know what will work! I will hire false witnesses to testify against Naboth. If they testify that Naboth is a blasphemer and that he cursed God and the king, then there is legal ground to stone him!

Jezebel was on a roll. Her mind continued to spin a wicked web of reprisal and destruction.

I will use religion to convince them that this is an honorable deed. I will proclaim a fast; those people are really into fasting and praying. They will never suspect I have tricked them!

Yes, by proclaiming a fast the magistrates will understand the seriousness of the charge against Naboth. I will convince them that if they do not destroy this blasphemer, then their God will judge their city. Surely they will remember the religious myth that their God destroyed an entire nation because of the sin of one man, Achan. They will think that by destroying the accursed person, their city will not be cursed. What fools they are!

Thoughts and schemes were coming faster than Jezebel could pen. Hurriedly she wrote instructions to the magistrates to proclaim the fast. *Whom shall I hire to falsely accuse Naboth?*

Jezebel recalled meeting two men, the sons of Belial. She was wickedly delighted as she remembered how easily they seemed to defile any atmosphere. They were truly ancestors of Belial, sons of the devil himself, cloaked with wickedness and perversion.

"Oh, yes! They will be perfect for this job!" she shouted with excitement. "Why, even their ancestors are blasphemers, liars and false accusers. I can count on them to do anything for money. Justice will be served against Naboth by ordering that he be taken out of the city and stoned to death!"

Finishing her instructions, Jezebel grabbed the king's privy seal. She had already assumed self-appointed power when she had used her husband's seal to slay the prophets, so it was easy for her to do it again. After forging the king's name to each letter, Naboth's fate of death was sealed.

When the magistrates received their instructions, they carried out the wicked plans of Jezebel. A fast was proclaimed, and they brought Naboth before the people. The sons of Belial were paraded before the people, and they falsely testified that Naboth had blasphemed God and the king. With legal grounds for the sentence of death, they carried Naboth out of the city and stoned him.

Jezebel anxiously waited for the news of Naboth's death. When word was sent to her that the evil deed was accomplished, the queen approached her husband immediately with the news that he was now the owner of Naboth's vineyard.

Not even asking how, what or why, Ahab rose up, went down to the vineyard and took possession. Smiling as he walked, Ahab said to himself, *I knew I could count on Jezebel to get what I needed. She really is an amazing woman.*

Jezebel's Plans of Destruction Are the Same Today

Just as Jezebel planned and schemed to steal Naboth's inheritance, the demonic force of Jezebel devises plots to steal our promises today. This principality wars relentlessly to steal our future. Operating through illegitimate authority, the demonic force of Jezebel attempts to negate every prophecy and promise we have received from the Lord. We will discuss more about this later, but for now we are going to focus on how Jezebel desires to steal our future and our inheritance.

Naboth cherished his inheritance. He valued his birthright and was not going to sell out to anyone, even for profit. Unlike Esau, who sold his birthright for a bowl of soup, Naboth understood the importance of remaining in possession of an inheritance. Likewise, we should value what God has spoken in His Word concerning our future and our promise of success, breakthrough and victory. Though the enemy strategizes to seduce us to sell out and settle for less than what God has for us, we must remain determined never to allow the enemy to steal our blessing.

Your Inheritance Is Much More than a Vegetable Garden!

Now let's discuss the importance of receiving an inheritance. Two types of inheritances are biblical: the spiritual inheritance and the physical inheritance. According to patriarchal studies in Genesis, the firstborn son legally received the birthright, or inheritance, both physical and spiritual. In the absence of a son, another relation could become an heir.

The nation of Israel, God's firstborn, had the legal right to an inheritance from God. The Israelites physical inheritance was the land of Canaan. Their spiritual inheritance was the blessing passed down to them as God's chosen people, descendants of Abraham, Isaac and Jacob. The land of Canaan, then, was only a portion of their inheritance, and interestingly, even today their battle for the land still exists. For centuries, the nation of Israel has been and is still warring over the land given to them by God.

Christians today have access to God's inheritance through adoption; we are not His firstborn but have become heirs through Christ's redeeming work on the cross. We refer to the *Promised Land* as our spiritual land of promise. It involves our future and all God has for us. Christ, as the Lamb slain, has given us victory over death, sickness and disease, and one day we will rule and reign over all our enemies (see Ephesians 1:3–18; Colossians 3:23–24; Hebrews 1:4; and 1 Peter 1:4).

Proverbs 13:22 says a wise parent leaves an inheritance for his children and future generations. It is a great blessing to receive an inheritance from loved ones. Not all people, however, fully understand the importance of an inheritance. Many parents do not consider it wise to save for the future and leave an inheritance. Even more sadly, many children do not position themselves to receive an inheritance. As previously mentioned, in a weak moment Esau, the son of Isaac, sold his inheritance to his brother, Jacob, for a bowl of soup. He sold his full inheritance, both physical and spiritual, because of a fleshly desire.

Dear ones, the enemy has the same plans today. The hordes of hell apply great pressure to cause God's children to give up our godly inheritance. Satan belittles the value of the inheritance and tries to convince each of us that our inheritance, the "land" God has promised, is good enough only for "vegetables"! He lurks in the shadows, waiting for a "weak moment" to take our blessings. He intimidates, lies, strategizes and manipulates circumstances to get us to surrender and run from what belongs to us.

Precious child of God, don't sell out for a vegetable garden! Don't sell your inheritance for a fleshly desire. You have been given a promise from the Lord. Be determined to hold on to what God has promised you. Don't allow the enemy to seduce you into letting go of all God has for your future. Stand firm in every promise and speak boldly to the enemy, "I will not sell my inheritance!" It is worth fighting for!

How Jezebel Operates Today

The demonic influence of Jezebel has not changed much over the last several thousand years. She still uses the same techniques in trying to steal the inheritance of God's people. Let's look at the different ways this evil principality operates.

Jezebel Uses Witchcraft

Now it happened, when Joram saw Jehu, that he said, "Is it peace, Jehu?" So he answered, "What peace, as long as the harlotries of your mother Jezebel and her witchcraft are so many?"

2 Kings 9:22

Jezebel often manifests through divination and witchcraft. These are her calling cards. Jezebel actually uses a spirit of divination for her inspiration.

To put it simply, divination is witchcraft. In Acts 16:18, Paul addressed a woman with the spirit of divination after she continued to cause much distraction. Paul addressed her false flattery and drawing attention to herself—a tactic of the Jezebel stronghold. Through spiritual discernment Paul identified the evil spirit and cast it out of her.

The demonic power of Jezebel is a manipulating, controlling, seducing force that uses flattering words to seduce and infiltrate our emotions. This evil force flatters with insincere compliments. A compliment can be wonderful—we all need compliments—but when a wrong motive is attached, it comes from a wrong spirit. The motives behind false flattery are manipulation and control (i.e., witchcraft).

The Hebrew word for "flattery" is *chalaq*, which means "to divide, (be) smooth and seductive." It is derived from a root word meaning "smooth, slippery and deceitful." These are characteristics of a snake, and we all know who the snake is! Not surprisingly, the Hebrew word for *serpent* is linked with divination.

If you sense that someone is falsely flattering you, then be cognizant of an ulterior motive and the underlying witchcraft at work. If I discern that a person has an impure motive and then he or she pours on the compliments, I become fully aware that a spirit of witchcraft is attempting to gain entrance and control. If allowed, Jezebel will take root and bring separation and division.

The division can manifest in many different ways. Since Jezebel loves to teach, for example, she attempts to gain position with motives to divide a congregation. With her false doctrines, she separates others from the Truth and persuades them to follow her. This can end in a church split.

Following are examples of words of flattery that should raise huge red spiritual flags of witchcraft:

- "You are the most wonderful teacher I know. No one teaches the Word like you. I could sit for hours and listen to your voice. Why, I would bet that even your own husband/wife/pastor does not realize how wonderful you are." Red alert! This spirit is falsely flattering you because it is attempting to bring division between a husband and wife or among leadership.

- "No one can prophesy like you. You have the most tremendous prophetic flow. I don't know why your pastor does not allow you to prophesy more. I think we should start our own prophetic church and teach others to follow the Spirit as we do." Red alert! This spirit is falsely flattering because it wants a position of authority. It is attempting to split a congregation and lead others into rebellion.

Let's face it, we feel great when someone compliments us. Jezebel knows that most of us enjoy hearing how wonderful we are, so she manipulates, controls and seduces us into her web of divination. She cannot control us unless she first seduces us with her witchcraft. Don't allow her tears, emotions and false flattery to open the doors of your soul.

Jezebel Uses False Prophecy

Witchcraft is not the only tool Jezebel uses to manipulate and gain control. She also uses false prophecy.

Her controlling manipulation especially targets spiritual authority and thrives on atmospheres of insecurity. Unfortunately many prophesies in the Church today are the result of a controlling and undermining Jezebel influence. I have observed this demonic power falsely prophesying

51

over others for monetary gain and self-promotion. Its delivery sounds "spiritual" or has a flamboyant punch to it; the Church therefore needs to judge carefully all prophetic utterances. Keep in mind that a person motivated by Jezebel does not easily submit to authority, oversight or correction, which is a rebellious response to the Lord's instruction (see Hebrews 13:17, 1 John 4:1).

While pastoring a church in Texas we experienced many witchcraft attacks from a Jezebel stronghold. Our church had a strong apostolic/prophetic ministry with a mandate to fulfill Ephesians 4:11–12 in training and equipping the saints, especially in the prophetic ministry. We were a prime target for Jezebel, who promotes and operates in false prophecy, attacking all true prophets and prophetic ministries. Our church experienced a horrendous attack from what I refer to as "sniper" maneuvers. In other words, Jezebel sent in a SWAT team to sow seeds of false prophecy. This resulted in many of us suffering from confusion, physical infirmities and strange diseases, such as unusual skin conditions with no medical explanation, and strange tumors that appeared and then disappeared.

Jezebel Operates with the Python Spirit

During this attack of Jezebel on our church in Texas, I sometimes personally felt as if the breath were being "squeezed out" of my lungs, and I feared for my life! Have you ever felt as I did, that the life and breath were being squeezed out of you? Maybe the enemy has attacked your finances and has squeezed out all you have possessed.

This could be the result of Jezebel and the python spirit. In his book, *Unmasking the Jezebel Spirit*, John Paul Jackson states, "The Jezebel spirit uses a spirit of divination, which in the Greek is called *python*."[3] A python snake is large and muscular and kills its prey by squeezing, or constricting, until the prey suffocates.

The python spirit is loosed whenever Jezebel is in the midst. It squeezes life out of hope, breakthroughs, finances and lives. It "constricts" us to the point that we are unable to move forward into our future. As the python constricts with every squeeze, we feel the restraints and therefore are contained in old patterns of behavior and hopelessness. This is one way Jezebel locks us down into our past with no hope for freedom.

Jezebel Quenches the Anointing

Not only does Jezebel desire to steal future inheritance and blessings, but this evil power also targets anointing. When our church experienced Jezebel's wrath, we called our leadership team together to fast and pray. It was time to expose the spirit to the congregation and defeat it. On the day I was to preach and expose the manifestations of Jezebel, I awoke with a sickening headache and could barely get out of bed. I struggled to get to church and felt weak and faint. As I began to preach, I became so confused I could barely speak. I heard the Lord say, *Jezebel has targeted your anointing. Do not allow her to seduce you into stopping. Rebuke the spirit, and I will empower you.* I knew that Jezebel has no power unless she is able to seduce us. If she can seduce us into believing her lies, then she gains the victory. The Lord reminded me that other manifestations of Jezebel's witchcraft were dizziness and confusion, so I asked the congregation to pray with me and rebuke the manifestation of Jezebel. Suddenly the dizziness and confusion left, and I was able to proceed with my message and expose the Jezebel stronghold.

Since Jezebel hates repentance (see Revelation 2:21), I was determined to defeat her tactics by leading the congregation in prayers of repentance. We began to ask the Lord to forgive us if we had ever tolerated that demonic power. Right in the middle of the prayer a woman in the congregation began to scream and falsely prophesy!

" 'Yea!' saith the Lord. 'I am not in this place! I am not in the dance; I am not in the prophetic ministry! I am not here.' " Then she fell to the floor and did not move, as if to persuade us that she had been slain by the power of God.

My husband, Mickey, and I looked at each other, both aware of the false voice. It was a Jezebel manifestation. *The nerve of that spirit!* I thought. I signaled to our ushers to help her stand up. I was getting angry now; here I was teaching against witchcraft and the assignments of Jezebel, and the spirit itself rose up and attempted to gain attention. How could a true prophet of God prophesy and proclaim, "I am not in the prophetic ministry" and "I am not here"? If God was not prophesying, then who was? Obviously, the enemy!

Amazingly, the woman indicated after the service that she wanted to join our church! Now why would she want to join a church where she did not believe God to be? Mickey and I knew that Jezebel is attracted to a true prophetic ministry. We asked her to commit to our new members class and some counseling. At first she squirmed, searching for all types of excuses as to why she could not attend the classes, and then came the big question, "Why do I need counseling?"

Finally I had an open door to speak truth to her. I explained that I had discerned she was operating in confusion and that she had experienced periods of rejection. I tried to be loving and helpful as I continued to minister to her through the word of knowledge and prophetic insight. The anointing was upon me as I spoke truth. The Holy Spirit ministered to her, and she began to weep uncontrollably. After some intense ministry, she submitted to counseling and deliverance.

I wish I had a good report to share. During ensuing deliverance sessions, the woman refused to repent and continued to make excuses for her behavior. She accepted no responsibility for her actions and continued to blame others. After her sessions she phoned church members to complain about our "lack of anointing," and she manipulated other members to feel sorry for her. She made her way onto our intercessory team and attempted to control the prayer meetings. During intercession she supposedly received direction from God as to how the church finances were to be spent and who were really called as leaders. And though she had not continued her deliverance sessions, she wrote letters about how God wanted deliverance sessions for others in the church!

I am still in shock as I remember how many of our congregation this woman deceived. Her group of sympathizers rallied to her defense as we spoke more truth. She lied about me, other leaders and anyone who tried to speak truth to her. She even attempted to drive a wedge between Mickey and me. One of Jezebel's seductions is to target the senior leader and seduce that person into believing her lies. This is especially dangerous if the Jezebel is a female and she targets a male leader who is married. Because my husband

and I have a strong commitment to each other, there was no way that this Jezebel was allowed to bring division between us, but that did not stop her from trying.

After I confronted the woman for lying to my husband and others, she left the church. If she had not left on her own, we were going to ask her to leave. We had desperately tried to help her receive healing and restoration, but because of her constant resistance and lack of repentance we knew that she had to leave. It took months to clean up the messes she had caused and to expose fully the lies she had concealed. Remember that Jezebel is linked to the occultic spirit, which keeps things "hidden." Only after much prayer and spiritual warfare were the hidden things revealed and the negative effects eradicated from our midst.

Looking back, I realize that those times of confronting the Jezebel spirit were the most difficult seasons. Jezebel tried to quench the anointing God had put upon our ministry. If His Holy Spirit had not revealed to us the work of this destructive spirit, it could have succeeded in its mission. Praise God, it did not!

Jezebel Seeks an Ahab

The Jezebel spirit always seeks an Ahab with which to align. Some have labeled Ahab a wimp because Jezebel overpowered him. Ahab was, however, able to control through his ability to irritate and provoke—a silent and passive control. I believe a psychologist might refer to this as being "passive-aggressive." The Scripture says that Ahab "did more to provoke the LORD God of Israel to anger than all the kings of Israel that were before him" (1 Kings 16:33, KJV).

Ahabs have the ability to use their Jezebel wives (or friends or relationships) to do their dirty work. An Ahab easily "hides behind the skirts of Jezebel" to do his evil bidding. (I use this phrase metaphorically, as neither the strongholds of Ahab nor Jezebel has gender.) An Ahab will provoke us to anger and cause us to remain defensive. Be on guard—Ahab is sneaky! Jezebel was intimidating and an in-your-face person; therefore, many with a personality like Ahab submit to her direct confrontations. Jezebel and Ahab spirits "team up" to gain control of a situation.

Ahab knew better than to marry an idol worshiper, but his lust for power overrode his commitment to God. Though Ahab was justified in his own eyes, God condemned Ahab for his apostasy, for "no one else so completely sold himself to . . . evil . . . as did Ahab, for his wife, Jezebel, influenced him" (1 Kings 21:25, NLT).

Manifestations of Jezebel

Now that we have looked at what the demonic force of Jezebel does, let's take a look at some of her characteristics. In this way we can better identify her when she targets an individual person, business or ministry. Some wonderful books go into great detail about the many different ways this spirit manifests, but I will list the opposition I have encountered personally. The Jezebel spirit typically:

- Will not submit. Jezebel's name means "non-cohabitation," indicating that she is independent and self-serving and will not cohabit with anyone, especially authority figures.

57

- Is seductive in nature. The spirit seduces others through the tactics of false flattery, control and manipulation. It also will use sexual seduction if possible.
- Pits one person against another, especially leader against leader and husband against wife.
- Infiltrates intercessory prayer ministry. The spirit specifically targets intercession in order to release witchcraft prayers. It tries to gain control so it can direct the prayers, and this is witchcraft.
- Prides itself on seeming "more spiritual" than others.
- Hooks others with "emotionalism."
- Manipulates others through false dreams and visions.
- Uses flattering words.
- Seeks opportunities to teach. The spirit desires to gain a platform so that it can operate in its perverted illegitimate power and control.
- Twists Scripture.
- Infiltrates prophetic ministry and falsely prophesies. Jezebel is attracted to prophecy and attempts to prophesy falsely if allowed. She operates through divination and witchcraft rather than through the pure gift of prophecy. Jezebel "calls herself" a prophetess; that is, God does not acknowledge her prophetic gifting (see Revelation 2:20).
- Brings with it a spirit of infirmity.
- Hinders praise and worship.
- Causes financial lack. Jezebel attacks any finances that she cannot control. If a person who is influenced by the demonic power of Jezebel, for example, disagrees with the way church finances are allotted, the spirit

58

exercises controlling prayers and attitudes concerning the situation. Anytime Jezebel does not get her way, especially in finances, the spirit manifests. Once the spirit is dealt with, the finances increase!

What the Lord Says about Jezebel

Jezebel is mentioned in both the Old and New Testaments. In Revelation 2:18–21 the Lord specifically addresses the evil, seductive powers of Jezebel and her adverse effect on His church in Thyatira. Though Jezebel was long since dead, the spirit in which she operated was still influencing the churches, and this was what God was addressing. Jezebel had introduced idolatrous worship, led His servants astray and encouraged them into sexual sin. He warned the church members that if they continued to tolerate her evil seductions, He would strongly discipline them. The Lord rebuked anyone who tolerated her evil plans and maneuvers.

"Nevertheless I have a few things against you, because you allow that woman Jezebel, who calls herself a prophetess, to teach and seduce My servants to commit sexual immorality and eat things sacrificed to idols. And I gave her time to repent of her sexual immorality, and she did not repent. Indeed I will cast her into a sickbed, and those who commit adultery with her into great tribulation, unless they repent of their deeds. I will kill her children with death, and all the churches shall know that I am He who searches the minds and hearts. And I will give to each one of you according to your works."

Revelation 2:20–23

59

Dear ones, when God begins to point out a specific fault, we had better listen! The Lord specifically warned the church in Thyatira of her sin. Though the church was commended for its positive qualities, God brought His correction concerning the church's toleration of Jezebel.

It is true that this warning was written to a specific church in the city of Thyatira, but the needed adjustment holds true today for every church, ministry, minister and layperson. Jezebel's spirit—the way the evil realm uses her tactics—is still in operation today, and God detests our toleration of this evil influence.

According to Revelation 2:20–28, the Lord says this about Jezebel:

1. She calls herself a prophetess (see verse 20)—but is not!

2. She teaches and seduces God's servants to commit fornication (see verse 20). Fornication is not just sexual sin. The term refers to desiring anything before its time, thus aborting the proper timing of things. The desire is active because one knows that it will eventually happen, but the Jezebel spirit convinces us that we have to have it now.

3. She teaches God's servants to eat things sacrificed to idols (see verse 20). Eating foods sacrificed to idols is what I refer to as "eating the devil's words." We must guard our ears and partake only of what God says concerning our situations and us.

4. Jezebel hates repentance (see verse 21). She blocks repentance in a congregation through selfish and self-centered prayers, usually rooted in jealousy, and by

causing offenses. Offenses against each other open doors to death structures.

5. Those who come into agreement with Jezebel suffer great tribulation (see verse 22). Oh, my! This is the part I do not like to discuss. I grieve over what happens when one agrees with this evil stronghold. The word *tribulation* translates as "affliction, trouble, anguish, persecution; burdened; a pressing, pressure; distress, suffering, oppression; narrow; and pressed hard upon." When we come into agreement with the seduction of Jezebel, we allow demonic entrance, resulting in affliction, trouble and distress.

6. The spirit of death operates in conjunction with Jezebel (see verse 23). The Lord says He will put Jezebel's children to death. We will discuss this in the next chapter when we study Athaliah, her daughter, but for now we need to recognize that those who make a covenant with the ways of Jezebel are targeted by the spirit of death. The spirit of death causes not only premature death, but also fear, torment and death to vision.

Words of Warning

Certain words are signs that you may be entering the combat zone with Jezebel. If you have heard others make statements similar to the following examples, then those people have been partially or strongly influenced by Jezebel, and you need to prepare for battle:

- "I was so wounded and mistreated in my last church. No one ever recognized my potential." This may indicate that the person was being corrected for improper behavior and would not submit to authority.

- "I feel God sent me here to help you. I know I just became a member, but I have a teaching gift. When can I start?" The Word states that your gift will make room for you. When someone is pushing his or her way into position, it is always a red flag.

- "God sent me here to be your friend, someone you can confide in." I have learned to run in the opposite direction when I hear that one! Trust takes time, and a person with a pure motive will wait for God's timing in a relationship.

- "No one ever recognizes my gifts." In other words, I want to have a position of authority, and no one will give it to me!

- "I have a prophetic gift and no one allows me to prophesy on their prophetic teams." Most of the time a person influenced by Jezebel will not receive correction concerning false words he or she gave. Because Jezebel is often rooted in rejection, one influenced with this demonic force will receive correction as rejection.

- "No one understands me." Jezebel wants everything her way. If there is any opposition or correction, then it is always someone else's fault. The person is deceived into believing that everyone is against him or her.

- "The pastors will not take time to help me." Many times we have attempted to give godly counsel, but Jezebel would walk away, refusing to be healed. Blaming others for the lack of submission and repentance was the counterattack against godly authority.

The Power of Repentance

Sometimes we are blinded to the seductions of Jezebel attempting to work through us. While you have been reading, has the Holy Spirit illuminated an area where you may have allowed an entrance to the Jezebel influence? Why don't you take a few moments right now to examine your life? Do you identify with any of Jezebel's tendencies? At times do you control, or are you easily controlled? Maybe you have been too passive and allowed Jezebel to influence your decisions. If you feel the Holy Spirit tugging at your heart, then He wants to illuminate the truth and lead you into repentance.

Repentance is one of our weapons against the enemy. Remember that Jezebel hates repentance. When Jesus addressed the church of Thyatira, He said He gave Jezebel the opportunity to repent, but she did not. Jezebel sets us up to refuse opportunities to repent. We should not repent to the Lord for our sin and then harbor resentment and unforgiveness in our hearts. Often we are stubborn and refuse to open our spiritual eyes to the truth concerning our sinful behavior. Many times we harbor resentment and bitterness because of unjust treatment from the past, such as a stolen inheritance, lies or slander. Unconfessed bitterness can steal joy and breakthroughs. It can even cause us to lose future blessings (see Hebrews 12:15–18).

True repentance involves change—especially changing the mind. All through this book you will have opportunity to repent to the Lord for allowing the enemy any place in your life. If the Spirit of God pricks your heart during any of the teachings in this book, please take some private time with the Lord. Repentance always releases you to become transformed and renewed by His divine Spirit.

Please do not wait until the end of a chapter to stop and talk to the Lord. Whenever the Holy Spirit prompts, take a few moments and discuss your situation with Him. Repent and pray. When we repent, the Lord is merciful and quick to forgive.

Correction is not rejection. When God corrects, He does not reject. "For whom the LORD loves He corrects" (Proverbs 3:12). His desire is for us to fulfill our destinies. It is Satan who wants us to feel rejected, who desires to steal blessings, inheritance and destiny.

I encourage you to take a few moments and list the different ways Satan has applied pressure. Then repent for believing his lies or submitting to his tactics by praying the prayer below:

Heavenly Father, I need Your Holy Spirit to lead me into all truth. I am determined never to allow my inheritance to be stolen. It is my desire to fulfill my entire destiny and experience a life of fullness and increase. I lay aside every fear that might tie me to my past. I choose not to give heed to the lies of the enemy. I am determined to be a mature believer and grow past all childish thoughts and actions. Forgive me for every area where I have given place to control and manipulation and the influence of a Jezebel spirit. I close every door to Satan. From this day forward I choose not to listen to the lies of the enemy. I let go of all bitterness from unjust treatment. I put on the full armor of God, which protects me from the enemy's evil plans of destruction. I claim the promises in Psalm 91:14–15, which states that because I have set my love on You, You will deliver me and set me on high. I can trust that as I call upon Your holy name, You will answer me. You will be with me in times of trouble, deliver me and honor me. In the name of Jesus, Amen.

Whatever you have experienced, God is able to redeem your past. Don't get discouraged and stop reading this book! You will become even more empowered to defeat the enemy as you continue to move forward into greater revelation.

3

The Gods of Jezebel

You shall have no other gods before Me. . . . You shall not
bow down to them nor serve them.

Exodus 20:3, 5

Jezebel is labeled a harlot, an adulteress and one who operated in witchcraft (see 2 Kings 9:22). She is depicted as
someone who was controlling, manipulating, scheming,
sexually promiscuous, perverted and an idol worshiper.
How in the world could someone become so evil? Through
her devoted allegiance to her idols, evil spirits took over
Jezebel's life and became a controlling influence. Her every
motivation was satanically inspired.

People become like the gods they serve. Just as Christians
become more Christlike because they worship Him, others

become a mirror image of the idol to which they bow. One can, therefore, tell a lot about biblical characters by identifying their gods. By carefully studying the idols they revered, we gain insight into lifestyles, behavior patterns and belief systems and are able to surmise the reasons for the biblical characters' personalities, motivations and character flaws. To more fully understand the manifestations of Jezebel, then, we need to closely examine her gods, as well as those of her family. In this way we will learn ways to contend successfully with this evil power and destroy her evil influence.

It would be beneficial to get a red pen or marker, as God will reveal areas of idolatrous worship that you may not be aware you have embraced. Feel free to mark every page where the Lord reveals an iniquitous pattern in your life. Remain open and read slowly. Ask Him to open your heart, eyes and ears so that you can be totally free from Jezebel's influence. Dog-ear every page that ministers to you, journal, or use different-colored markers to identify prayer targets for the end of each chapter. You have permission to mark up this entire book if necessary—I want you free indeed!

Jezebel Brought Her Gods with Her

Jezebel's name translates as "unhusbanded." Although married, she would never fully submit to her husband, signifying that the true significance of a marriage was not important. Her marriage to Ahab was a political arrangement. Ahab's father, Omri, was Israel's sixth king. He sealed an alliance with Phonecia through the marriage of his son to Jezebel, the daughter of Ethbaal, king of the Sidoneans. The alliance brought a peace treaty. But this was not just a treaty between two nations; it was a treaty with idolatry. When Ahab married Jezebel, she brought not only her alliance but also her idol worship to Israel.

Jezebel set up idol worship and prostitution in the temples. For years Israel had struggled with her idolatrous lifestyle. Now, because of political protocol, Israel was ceremonially required to respect the religious beliefs of Ahab's wife.

This is a prime example of what will happen if our political system embraces Jezebel! The devil moves right in and takes over, and soon it becomes "politically correct" to compromise and embrace all levels of spiritual idolatry. The Jezebel influence convinces us that being "politically correct" is more important than being "godly obedient."

Let's take a deeper look at the idols Jezebel introduced to the Israelites and how they affected them—and how the spirits behind them still affect us today.

Baal: A False God

Did you notice the name *Baal* embedded in Jezebel's father's name, Ethbaal? Baal was the male Phoenician god, and Jezebel's father's name spoke of the family idolatry. *Ethbaal* means "like unto Baal," indicating that her father took on the likeness or characteristics of the god he worshiped. Studying Baal gives us greater insight into the person and spirit of Jezebel.

Baal was the principal male god of the Phoenicians and was symbolized as a calf or bull. Exodus 32 documents the history of the influence of Baal on the Israelites. When Moses delayed descending from Mount Sinai, where God was giving him the Ten Commandments, his absence generated fear among the people and caused them to waver. They coveted a god that would go before them (see verse 1). They desired a leader who was with them at all times. The Israelites beheld Moses as a "god" whom they could touch and see so that they would feel secure. So they approached Aaron and insisted that he make an idol for them to worship—a god they could see in the natural. They said to Aaron, "Come, make us gods. . . . We do not know what has become of [Moses]" (verse 1).

Instead of taking authority in his priestly office and turning their hearts toward the Lord and His purposes, Aaron agreed with the people. He had them bring their jewelry, and he made a golden calf in the image of Baal. They mocked God, drank and played. Then they bowed down and worshiped the image of Baal, proclaiming it as their god. The Lord sent Moses back to deal with the rebellious Israelites, and His anger burned against them. He said they had become a stiff-necked people.

How Baal Operates

The history of the Israelites' worship of Baal offers insight into the characteristics of this god:

- First, Baal and the evil powers at work behind it promote rebellion. They encourage conspiracies against godly leaders. Remember that Satan was cast down from heaven because of his rebellion against God and his negative influence on one-third of the angels.
- Second, Baal causes people to become impatient and unwilling to wait on God's timing.

- Third, the demonic forces behind Baal cause God's people to doubt the abilities of God and Moses to lead. When rebellion sets in, Satan uses it to cause people to doubt the leaders God has put over them.
- Fourth, the people commit sin, turn from God and make and bow down to a false idol.
- Fifth, they eat, drink, rise up and play. In this instance, the word *play* means "to laugh and mock God."
- Sixth, the people turn aside from God's direction.
- Finally, they become a stiff-necked people. *Stiff-necked* means "stubborn."

Stiff-Necked and Rebellious

The book of Acts presents the New Testament description of Israel's rebellion against Moses and God:

Our ancestors were unwilling to obey him; instead, they pushed him aside, and in their hearts they turned back to Egypt, saying to Aaron, "Make gods for us who will lead the way for us; as for this Moses who led us out from the land of Egypt, we do not know what has happened to him." At that time they made a calf, offered a sacrifice to the idol, and reveled in the works of their hands. But God turned away from them and handed them over to worship the host of heaven, as it is written in the book of the prophets: "Did you offer to me slain victims and sacrifices forty years in the wilderness, O house of Israel?"

Acts 7:39–42, NRSV

When the people demanded to have a god they could "see," the idolatry brought such a spirit of deception that

God turned away. Their rebellion caused God to give them over to darkness, death and the idols they served. What a horrible thought! How tormenting it would be to know that God would actually turn away and deliver us into Satan's hands!

Like the Israelites, many of us today remain stiff-necked and rebellious. Let's not be rebuked by the Lord for remaining "stiff-necked and uncircumcised in heart and ears . . . resist[ing] the Holy Spirit. . . . And [as our fathers] kill[ing] those who foretold the coming of the Just One" (Acts 7:51–52). Dear ones, let's give God no reason to turn away and deliver us into the hands of our enemy!

We have a choice. God said, "I have set before you life and death, blessing and cursing: therefore choose life, that both thou and thy seed may live" (Deuteronomy 30:19, KJV). By choosing life we allow God to heal our hearts. If, however, we choose not to fully follow God, then we are choosing to remain stiff-necked and rebellious.

Baal Wants It Now!

The Israelites were angered by Moses' absence. They did not understand the intensity of Moses' calling, nor did they fully know where Moses was when they desired his presence. Offended, they assumed the worst, turning from God and His divine direction to bow to the evil influence of Baal.

The spirit behind Baal insists that we have "who" we want, "when" we want him and that he "do what" we want. This spirit is based upon performance, rather than relationship.

Today a similar thing occurs when a leader cannot immediately be available to a congregation. I am reminded of the years I pastored a local church and some complained when I was unable to immediately return a phone call or meet with them on the spur of the moment. Though I was legitimately unavailable at the time of the call, they wanted me right then. With multitudes of phone calls and e-mails, it is impossible to care for every need and expectation. Immaturity in the Body of Christ always dictates that a person meet an immediate need, rather than going "in person" to the real "need-meeter," Jesus.

Baal Uses False Accusations and Lies

The same evil spirit preys upon a congregation with false accusations and lies when a leader is absent and unable to defend himself or herself. Though the spirit of Jezebel has no gender, it mainly works through women; unfortunately women are more likely to gossip and have idle tongues. This provides a way for the evil spirit to access control through jealousy, competition or need for attention.

Baal Tries to Seize Authority Illegitimately

Tyre, where Ethbaal was king, was a city that was never conquered by the Israelites. Tyre was part of the Promised Land, but Israel never received the possession. It was historically noted as being a "strong" city (a stronghold!) and was also the merchant city for trade. Wealth and power belonged to the city. Ethbaal became king of Tyre only because he plotted murder and illegally seized the throne.

No wonder Jezebel was so ruthlessly determined to seize everything she lusted after! She was following in her father's footsteps. Her daughter, too, suffered from this generational root. Both Jezebel and Athaliah followed Ethbaal's lead by committing murder and illegally seizing the thrones of Israel and Judah.

The evil stronghold behind Baal, therefore, promotes an illegitimate seize of authority. This is the same stronghold behind a governmental *coup d'etat*—the seizing of the throne or authority through death, manipulation and/or control. I have actually spoken with male pastors who confessed that they knew of females in their congregations who prayed the pastors' wives would die. This was how much they wanted to become the next "Mrs. Pastor" of the congregation.

When Jezebel arises within a family, it seeks to usurp authority. In a business, it seeks power and manipulates to gain financial control. In a church, it seeks position and power, and it gossips, manipulates and even lies to gain spiritual authority. In a local community, the self-promoting spirit runs for political office with intent to gain authority and status. In all levels of government, the demonic force attempts to obtain power for selfish gain and to change laws to serve idolatrous beliefs. The demonic power of Jezebel, therefore, is the stronghold influencing the immorality in government, which leads to ungodly laws such as legalized abortion, same-sex marriage and abolishing prayer in schools.

The devil tries to persuade us to complain about our leaders, rather than take spiritual responsibility and action. We would gain more spiritual ground if we would pray for God's divine government to be manifested upon the earth instead of murmuring and complaining about the economy and political policies. God *is* government. He does not come into agreement with our political structure; He requires us to agree with Him and His divine order. Any political attempt to overthrow what He has ordained in government is a Jezebel assignment of immorality and illegitimate authority.

Baal Promotes a Religious Spirit

Jezebel had an abundance of religious zeal. She was so religious and devoted to Baal that she introduced idolatry to her husband, King Ahab, and then established a religious platform for false prophets in Israel. She took her idols into the Jewish temples and erected them in the high places of the city. She even used the cloak of religion to manipulate the city officials as she called for a holy "fast" to do her evil deeds. She was one of the most committed evangelists known in biblical history, as she was religiously zealous to evangelize her entire community and convert the entire nation to her gods. Jezebel was strongly motivated in her worship, so much so that she had many of God's prophets murdered. Jezebel was driven to expel any opposition to her god, going to extreme measures to establish him as the only one to be worshiped in all Israel. She did all this in the name of "religion"!

The spirit behind Baal worship seduced the Israelites into believing that religious acts were the key to being spiritual. This is a "religious spirit"—one that promotes dead works and believes that "doing" is more important than "being." A spirit of religion requires constant outward expressions of loyalty rather than an inward, heartfelt desire to serve. This spirit is characterized by an unhealthy drive to prove oneself through demonstration and commitment rather than expressing true love and devotion through intimate worship. The commitment is based upon performance rather than relationship.

Many people today have the same type of religious zeal, and it is the spirit of Baal that influences them. The religious spirit causes people to become extremely legalistic and dogmatic in their religious views. In the same way that Jezebel was controlling, this spirit seeks control wherever there is an authority structure. If Jezebel is in operation in a local church, for example, a pastor or leader may exert so much control that the Spirit of God is not allowed to minister to the congregation. Also, many times the worship becomes a religious "tradition" rather than an avenue of glorifying God. Jezebel perverts the true worship of God and turns it into rules, regulations and laws.

How many times have we witnessed crimes involving Christian leaders? Some leaders have compromised Christian standards and morality because the evil powers of Jezebel have seduced them away from true holiness and godly character. Recently we have heard, for example, of priests molesting children. And yet, when proper church discipline is needed, little or no discipline is applied. Jezebel's religious spirit of Baal convinces us that we should have mercy and overlook the injustice done. True justice involves righteous discipline, yet we compromise the standard of holiness and continue to allow injustice by turning the other cheek when godly standards are needed. Remember that it was Jezebel who used religion to murder Naboth; she called a religious fast to get her deed accomplished. How often do we also say, "God told me to do that" as an excuse for not being accountable to remain holy and pure in our deeds and intentions? I truly believe in God's mercy and restoration, but restoration usually requires adjustment.

In the same way it seduced the Israelites, Baal, the strongest spirit behind Jezebel, attempts to seduce us into believing that religious acts are the key to being spiritual. We must be ready to confront this religious spirit and keep it from turning us away from righteousness.

Baal Is the God of Performance

In 1 Kings 18 Elijah confronted Baal's false prophets. They expected their false god to speak to them, so they cried out and demonically manifested in a religious frenzy. The false prophets cut themselves so that blood gushed as they prophesied until the end of the day, attempting to get attention from this dead idol. In fact, it was their custom to express themselves in this fashion as they worshiped Baal:

> So they cried aloud, and *cut themselves, as was their custom,* with knives and lances, until the blood gushed out on them. . . . They prophesied. . . . But there was no voice; no one answered, no one paid attention.
>
> 1 Kings 18:28–29, emphasis mine

All attempts to be noticed by Baal were in vain. The outward expressions of these false prophets were all performance and no relationship.

It is the same for many of us today. When idolatry and the spirit of Baal are active, we feel we must perform correctly and do what is "customary." We may not be cutting ourselves to get God's attention, but we may feel pressure to perform so God will visit us and answer our need.

We have regulations and rules, for example, that govern our church services. Often we feel that we have to prophesy a certain way, sing certain songs in a particular order, take up offerings "properly"—all in an attempt to look right to God and others. Unless the idols of Baal are torn down, we will continue to perform for God rather than seek an intimate relationship with Him.

Baal's Titles

Baal was known as the "god of the heavens." He is the god of horoscope (an ability to "go before" and tell the future), the Ouija board and all false prophecy and divination.

Baal also was known as "the exalted lord of the earth" and "lord of the city." These titles reflect Baal's assignments over cities, nations and the earth. If a city is sinful, then the entire municipality might be isolated from God's blessings. An entire region might be barren because of Baal or idol worship.

Have you ever visited or ministered in a city and felt your prayers never penetrated the heavens but instead fell back to the earth, unfruitful? According to Deuteronomy 28:23, "Thy heaven . . . shall be brass, and the earth . . . shall be iron" (KJV) as the result of idolatry, sin and rebellion. When a people are disobedient, God shuts off heaven's blessings and causes the ground to be barren. Baal can therefore become a ruling principality over their city or region.

If the spirit of Jezebel is allowed to operate within a city, region or even local churches, you can bet on this one thing: Baal is active! Wherever Jezebel is given a place, she brings idol worship with her. As a result, a curse of barrenness and desolation takes root. But if we serve the Lord and worship only Him, then we receive His abundant blessings.

Baal's Associates: Molech and Rephan

An associate is someone with whom one does business. Their names become associated. Many times associates have strong covenant arrangements.

Demonic spirits are connected by their associations. They are associated with each other through their different "assignments." Fear and torment, for instance, work strongly together and associate with spirits of infirmity. When a person is ill, fear and torment are attached to the illness. Another example can be seen in how closely idolatry is linked with seducing and unclean spirits. In the temples of Baal (idolatry), sexual perversion and temple prostitution were common.

Acts 7:43 documents the various associates of Baal: the shrine of Molech, and the star god Rephan. The idols of Molech and Rephan, therefore, were associates of Baal. These false gods were worshiped among the countrymen of Jezebel.

In this chapter of Acts, the Lord confronted the Israelites and their idolatrous worship of Molech and Rephan. He said that the Israelites had carried these idols in their hearts rather than worshiping Him. While in the wilderness, they had set up a tabernacle in their hearts for these false idols instead of fully submitting to Him. The evil influence of Baal, Molech and Rephan upon the Israelites is apparent and explains why they were never able to fully cross over into their promise.

Molech (also known as Moloch) was the god of child sacrifice (see Jeremiah 19:5; 32:35). It was a murdering stronghold that took the lives of future generations. The influence of Baal and Molech more easily explain the spiritual dynamics motivating Jezebel to murder God's prophets. Subsequently, her generational seed, Athaliah, murdered her own grandsons to seize the throne of Judah.

Today, Molech is one of the evil spirits behind abortion in our society. Abortion is an ongoing atrocity, and it generates from a strong Jezebel influence. The seducing strongholds of Jezebel and Molech instigate violent crimes against innocent babies, and this has never been more obvious than during *Roe v. Wade*, when the lives of future generations hung in the balance. The spirit behind *Roe v. Wade* was the same spirit behind Jezebel and her generation (through Athaliah). It seeks to murder and destroy many future godly seeds and their inheritance.

Abortion is not limited to murdering unborn children. Abortion is the murder of all potential. In other words, whatever God has planned to be "birthed" can easily become aborted when Jezebel and her god Molech have influence.

Baal's other associate, the false god Rephan, was the idol worshiped secretly by the Israelites during their time in the wilderness. The name *Rephan* is translated as "lifeless." We all know that idols are lifeless since they can neither speak nor hear. But the name *Rephan* also indicates a curse of death associated with this idol. The entire time the Israelites carried these idols, attempting to hide their sin, they remained in bondage to their Egyptian lifestyle, which only brought more grief, sorrow and death. Is it any wonder that they were never allowed to cross over into their Promised Land? Every one of the adult Israelites, with the exception of Joshua and Caleb, died in the wilderness. Because they would not let go of their past, God had to raise up an entirely new generation to cross the Jordan and possess the land.

Dear ones, if we truly want to cross over into our places of promise, we cannot allow our past sins to be kept "secret." If we hide and hold on to our past sins, we will simply take these idolatrous acts from place to place and remain in bondage. Let's decide today, right now, to repent and change!

Baal's Bride: Ashtoreth

Besides being devoted to Baal worship, Jezebel also worshiped and served the goddess Ashtoreth. Jezebel, the seducer and manipulator, convinced Ahab to build altars to both of her idols. Through her devoted worship, therefore, Jezebel became one and the same as both idols, Ashtoreth and Baal.

Remember that we can tell a lot about a person by the idols he or she serves. Ashtoreth had a number of other titles, and each one reveals something about the characteristics of Jezebel:

- The Queen of Heaven/The Bride of Heaven
- The Goddess of Good Fortune
- The Goddess of Holiness
- The Goddess of Sex
- The Goddess of War
- Astarte
- Ishtar
- Ashtart
- Asherah
- Aphrodite[4]

Baal was considered the male god of heaven, and Ashtoreth was the female queen of heaven and bride of heaven. Worshiping these idols causes the heavens to become brass and the ground infertile. These two strongholds cause heaven's plans to become thwarted and delay spiritual breakthroughs. In addition, since Ashtoreth was allegedly married to Baal, the two strongholds work together to promote sexual perversion, human sacrifice, murder and slander against legitimate authority.

The spirit behind the idol of Ashtoreth promotes the feminist movement. Though I firmly believe that women should be promoted if they have the proper credentials and credibility, I do not embrace the Jezebel manipulation and offensive demonstrations represented by the leaders and members of feminist organizations.

The Ashtoreth stronghold promotes not only the activist movement for women but also such sins as abortion, homosexuality, same-sex marriages and pornography. Ashtoreth was worshiped in temples with both male and female prostitution. Sexual rites were connected to her worship, as well as eating the foods sacrificed to idols (the deceptive words of the devil). Idolatry eventually leads to sexual degeneration and perversion (see Colossians 3:5).

We can give the spirit of Jezebel and her association with Ashtoreth credit for much of the immorality in our society and culture today. Pornography and immorality among individuals, including ministers of the Gospel, are at red-alert levels. The more we tolerate the evil influence of Jezebel, the more influence from her idol worship is embraced.

Baal, Ashtoreth and the Occult

Both Baal and Ashtoreth are linked with occultic powers. Baal is a false prophetic spirit of divination, and Ashtoreth is a goddess of fortune (fortune-telling). The two gods were considered married—in covenant together—which is the closest possible association. Their teamwork releases a "double whammy" of demonic activity.

Motivated and controlled by the evil spirits to whom she bowed, Jezebel was steeped in the occult. Her involvement with Baal and Ashtoreth led to so much wickedness that God turned her over to her own lusts and perversion, ultimately leading to her destruction.

If you have an idolatrous nature, or if you have a history of idolatry in your family generations, then you can be assured you will be attracted to the occult. If you or the generations before you dabbled in fortune-telling, Ouija boards or other areas of darkness, then you face the downfall of Jezebel unless you renounce and repent of this idolatry. God does not tolerate the occult, for it is one of the worst forms of idolatry.

Jezebel's Gods Reveal Her Influence

We have now looked at the gods Jezebel worshiped: Baal, Molech, Rephan and Ashtoreth. We have seen that they operate in close association with one another, and we have discussed how their influences are evident today in such areas as abortion; child molestation and pornography; sexual perversion (including homosexuality, rape and molestation); the occult; demonic influence over an entire city, region or territory; religious spirits; death and premature death; and idol worship. In order to defeat Jezebel, we must remain mindful of the evil influence of each of these gods, which are still in operation today.

The Jezebel stronghold is more entrenched in the Church than ever before, and it is gaining political power. We must identify this evil spirit, pray against its tactics and eradicate it from our churches and government. To do this, we must start with ourselves.

4

CONFRONTING JEZEBEL

Ye are of God, little children, and have overcome them: because greater is he that is in you, than he that is in the world.

1 John 4:4, KJV

We can no longer tolerate the evil influence of Jezebel. If we continue to allow this evil power to operate, the driving force behind abortion, child pornography, the legalization of sexual perversion, increased crime, illegitimate authority and immorality will prevail. We have no alternative but to rise up and battle the occultic spirits behind Jezebel.

The Scriptures clearly discuss how displeased the Lord is if we "[permit] . . . Jezebel . . . to lead my servants astray" (Revelation 2:20, NLT). As we discussed, the church of Thyatira was rebuked for permitting Jezebel to seduce them into sexual sin and immorality. If we permit such actions today, then the Lord is also rebuking us.

The Lord promises to reward us if we refuse to tolerate Jezebel's influence, and He will empower us to effectively confront her. If you need empowerment and wisdom to confront a Jezebel spirit, then read on!

If It Is a War Satan Wants . . .

Remember that Ashtoreth is known as the goddess of war. She and all her associates are at war with the saints of God. The devil has declared an all-out attack to seduce God's children into spiritual apostasy.

As Christians, all of us are called to be in God's army. What is an army commissioned to do? It goes to war to defend a cause. Well, God is a God of war, and He has spoken to the warrior inside each of us. He has called us, His mighty army, to defend His cause. As believers and soldiers in God's army, we must rise up in our godly authority and declare war against the spirit of Jezebel and her idolatry.

Though the enemy may attempt to gather his troops, using his evil devices attached to the idol of Ashtoreth, the goddess of war, he will never be able to defeat God's mighty army. We are victorious through Christ Jesus! Gird up your loins, set your faces like flint toward your victory, choose life and renew your minds daily. The Word says that we are to "seek those things which are above. . . . Set [our affection] on things above, not on things on the earth" (Colossians 3:1–2).

As believers in Christ, we are instructed to rid ourselves of "fornication, uncleanness, inordinate affection, evil concupiscence, and covetousness, which is idolatry" (Colossians 3:5, KJV). Battling Jezebel, then, requires being cleansed from unrighteousness. We must put to death our fleshly desires and set our minds on heaven's plans in order to defeat the enemy.

Tearing Down vs. Bowing Down

In order to battle Jezebel we must tear down her false idols. As stated earlier, Jezebel was religious. She bowed down to false images and proved her loyalty to them by murdering the prophets of God. The Scripture speaks repeatedly about the evil process of "bowing down" to any god other than Jehovah. Exodus 23:24 gives specific instructions not to "bow down to their [false] gods ... but ... overthrow them." Exodus 20:5 states that if someone bows down to false idols, the iniquity of the sin is passed down to the third and fourth generations. In other words, there is a generational curse of iniquity because of the "bowing down" to any false god.

Iniquity is defined as "perverse and perverted, crooked, (to be) bowed down, troubled, wrong and wicked." The Hebrew word for *iniquity* is linked with the words that mean "twisted and bent." This implies that when one bows down, giving place to an idol, he or she has a "twisted" or "bent" belief system that is then passed from one generation to another.

In Scripture, whenever a godly leader was empowered with authority, one of the first demonstrations of his righteous leadership was to tear down the false idols. Gideon is a prime example. He was appointed by God as the commander of His army. But before commissioning, Gideon was instructed to tear down the idols in his family's backyard.

Gideon's family had worshiped Baal and Ashtoreth. To free himself and his family from the curse of iniquity, he was instructed to tear down the altars of these false gods and to rebuild the altar of God (see Judges 6:25–27). And then the false idol of Baal had to be completely destroyed in Israel before Gideon could lead the nation into victory. Their idolatrous worship had to be put to death first. It is the same today.

When an altar is built to the idol of Baal, Ashtoreth, Molech or any other false god, it is still an exaltation of the devil himself. The false image must be torn down to "dethrone" Satan from his seated position. If an idol is not torn down, then iniquity and iniquitous patterns are legally passed down from one generation to another. Satan has legal access to target a generation if he has not been dethroned. This is why entire nations are cursed with poverty and infirmity; they have bowed down to false images, and a death structure of iniquity is established.

We saw in chapter 1 that Revelation 2:12–13 addresses the seat of Satan in the city of Pergamos. The Lord was specifically addressing the Pergamos church for allowing Satan to remain "enthroned." He rebuked her inhabitants for their idolatry but said that He would forgive them if they repented of their sin. When we repent of sin, Satan is "dethroned" from his "seated position" over us, and God's throne is rebuilt.

Isn't that an awesome thought? Repentance removes Satan's legal hold (stronghold), and we are placed in right standing with the Lord as we make Him Lord over our lives. This is why Jezebel hates repentance!

We cannot defeat Jezebel and the demonic powers that influence her evil behavior without first tearing down Baal and establishing God's divine order upon the earth. To do spiritual warfare against Jezebel without binding the spirit of Baal is simply shadowboxing. The spirit behind Baal worship will remain active unless we cease from bowing down to any image other than the image of God. Every time we settle for less than what God says about us, we continue to bow down to Satan's destructive plans. Like Gideon, we must fully tear down the altars of false worship and rebuild the altars of God to have victory over evil influences. If false idols are not torn down and the enemy dethroned, then Satan still has legal access to oppress us.

Satan does not want to be dethroned from his power over us. The devil will not allow us to dethrone him without a fight. Gideon obeyed the Lord, but not without upsetting the city officials who threatened to kill him for tearing down their idols. These city officials believed that if the idols were destroyed, then certain death would befall them; after all, they believed Baal was their "divine protector." Well, if so, why were they still in bondage to their enemies? For years, the Midianites had stolen their grain at the threshing floors and caused them to live in fear, dread and hopelessness.

As we begin to tear down the altars of Baal and false worship, we will face opposition and evil oppression. The devil will try to make us fear his power, but we must remember who is really in control. Our God is bigger, and He will protect us—just as He did Gideon—when we advance boldly to destroy His enemies.

Idolatry Involves Heeding the Wrong Voice

You might be thinking, *I don't bow down to a false image.* Well, let's examine idolatry a little further.

To *bow down* means to give superiority or reverence to another being. In other words, we listen to the words of another being or honor another voice above God's. How many times have we listened to the voice of the enemy? How often do we heed what the devil says about us and exalt his words above what God has said? If we exalt Satan's words over God's, then we are bowing down to a *false image.* Dear ones, this is a form of idolatry!

Think about this for a minute. If God and His Word are one, then His Word is superior over any other words. If the devil is speaking his words over us and we embrace and believe them, then we exalt Satan's word above God, the Word. This is idolatry, plain and simple. When we believe what Satan says, we are bowing down to the false image.

Isaiah 46:2 states that when the Israelites bowed down to the false image, they were led into captivity. They remained in captivity for years, and the generations became paralyzed with iniquitous patterns due to the former idolatry. When there is idol worship in the land, it gives the devil legal entrance to adversely affect the generations. Dear ones, to protect our future seed, we need to stop bowing down to the words of the devil and rise up in great faith, embracing the Word of the Lord.

Submitting to Evil Powers behind the Idols

Now that we know idolatry involves a bowing down, we need to understand that when we bow down to any false image, we are submitting to the evil powers behind it. Any false belief system to which we submit empowers demonic activity against us. Buddha, for instance, has no power except when people believe the religious doctrines concerning the idol. When false, ungodly belief systems affect lifestyles, culture and religious activities, demons have legal access and entrance.

When Paul was in Ephesus, he confronted the demons behind the idolatrous worship. He stated that when a person worships idols, he or she is actually worshiping devils (see 1 Corinthians 10:19–20). The idols are helpless and can do nothing unless they are worshiped. As a result of false worship, demonic activity is released. The resulting effects in a church/community/city/family/government are sin, sexual perversion, crime, etc.

If we have embraced any image of God that is not truly who He says He is, then we are bowing down to a false image. If we do not truly believe, for example, that He is *Jehovah Jireh*, our Provider, and we constantly blame God for our poverty, then we have embraced and bowed to a false belief system, a false image of God. We therefore develop a twisted, perverted view of God that is not based upon His Word. As a result, our unbelief paves the way for us to remain in poverty and patterns of iniquity.

Though we may have "bowed down" to an image that is not God's character, God promises to forgive us and provide mercy. Even though you may notice a curse of iniquity in your generations, God's mercy can remove the curse. God revealed to Moses His attributes of mercy, graciousness and long-suffering and told him of His desire to forgive Israel for their iniquity:

> And the LORD passed before him and proclaimed, "The LORD, the LORD God, merciful and gracious, longsuffering, and abounding in goodness and truth, keeping mercy for thousands, forgiving iniquity and transgression and sin, by no means clearing the guilty, visiting the iniquity of the fathers upon the children and the children's children to the third and the fourth generation."
>
> Exodus 34:6–7

As God extended His mercy, Moses took immediate action and "bowed" before the Lord. He repented and asked God to forgive the sin of iniquity that brought a curse upon the generations (see Exodus 34:8–9). We must do the same thing today. We need to ask that His mercy forgive our ancestors, us and our generations for our sins and iniquities.

It Might Take a Wilderness

As we have discussed, the Philistines were strongly rooted in Baal and Dagon worship (we will discuss Dagon in more detail when we expose the spirit of Delilah in chapters 7 and 8). When the Israelites left Egypt, God knew they were not yet ready to confront the Philistines, as idolatry was still too deeply ingrained in them. If they had been confronted immediately with the defiling nature of the Philistines, then they would have lost the battle and been forced to return to Egypt: "God did not lead them on the road that runs through Philistine territory. . . . God said, 'If the people are faced with a battle, they might change their minds and return to Egypt'" (Exodus 13:17, NLT). The Israelites had not yet learned to fully trust God. And God knew it would take them forty years to trust Him enough that they would be fully prepared for battle. So He led them into the wilderness.

Similarly, we often wonder why God leads us into a wilderness. Many times we finally get free from a stronghold only to find ourselves in another wilderness experience! Could it be that this was the best route for us after leaving our previous "Egypt"? Maybe God knew this route was the best one, in case a Philistine stronghold of idolatry attempted to defile us. In the wilderness God proves our hearts, and we learn to fully trust Him.

Though the Israelites' itinerary would be longer through the desert, God knew the best course for their future—just as He knows the best course for each of us today. As we journey through the wilderness, God uses the necessary challenges to prove our hearts and strengthen our hands for war.

Confronting Those Influenced by Jezebel

Did God care about Jezebel? Absolutely! In fact, He gave her many opportunities to repent, but she never repented or turned from her immoralities (see Revelation 2:21). Does God care about those operating under Jezebel's evil influence today? Once again, absolutely! He is raising up believers and deliverance ministers to pray for those who are deceived by this evil spirit.

Some of you who are reading this book may find the need to confront someone influenced by Jezebel. Let's discuss

93

some effective ways to confront others oppressed by this stronghold.

First, never counsel or confront alone a person who operates under the influence of any seducing spirits. The spirits will manipulate and control to the point that the counselor becomes confused and disoriented. In particular, a male should never confront a female alone—I do not recommend this in *any* situation. A female Jezebel has tendencies to be seductive. Let me repeat: No male pastor or male leader should ever counsel a woman with Jezebel tendencies without additional counselors in the setting.

Second, pray before you counsel, and ask intercessors to pray during your confrontation. We have a team of intercessors praying before every confrontation and, if possible, during the session. If confronting a family, find someone in spiritual authority who can cover you in prayer during the confrontation so that the enemy has no place to interfere and cause confusion.

Third, ask for divine revelation concerning strongholds. Many times, I ask God for a dream concerning the person I counsel. Since Jezebel is linked strongly with an occultic spirit, she attempts to keep a great deal hidden. God is faithful to reveal the hidden strategies of the enemy so that I can counsel by His Spirit and see the person set free.

Fourth, keep a journal of every counseling session, including information you receive from other counselors and leaders. You will find a pattern of behavior and a common thread that will empower you as you confront the spirit's evil influence.

Finally, for pastors and counselors in particular, I advise you to tape-record the counseling session if possible. Tell the person that you are doing so for his or her protection and yours. The enemy has a way of twisting the words that are spoken, especially after a session.

Points to Consider in Confronting Jezebel

1. Don't be afraid of Jezebel! The Lord has given you a Scripture with a powerful punch: "Ye are of God, little children, and have overcome them: because greater is he that is in you, than he that is in the world" (1 John 4:4, KJV).

Do you see how big God is? Spend some time with Him today. Allow Him to show you His majesty and might. Study the lives of Abraham, Joseph, Joshua and Caleb. Examine how God proved His power to lead, deliver and encourage them. He desires to do the same for you. Write down your thoughts concerning God's ability to strengthen your faith.

2. The Lord says that no weapon Satan uses against us will prosper, and He says He will silence the tongue of our enemy (see Isaiah 54:17).

What weapons has the enemy recently hurled toward you? False accusations? Sickness and disease? Fear and intimidation? These are weapons that Jezebel uses against God's chosen. List Satan's weapons being used against you. Now write passages from Scripture that negate every weapon he has used. If you are battling fear, for example, then write 2 Timothy 1:7, which reads, "For God hath not given us the spirit of fear; but of power, and of love, and of a sound mind" (KJV). Then begin to declare God's Word against the enemy.

3. Submit yourself to the hand of God and ask for His empowerment to confront the Jezebel stronghold influencing your life. Tell the Lord you desire all that He has for you. Ask the Lord to begin to change you into His divine image. Rise up and declare His power to overcome!

Prayer to Dethrone Jezebel

Now is the time for you to repent, tear down your idols and dethrone Satan from his seated position:

Father God, I realize that I have allowed the evil powers that are behind Jezebel to affect my life. I have bowed down to a false image by not trusting in Your Word or believing that You are who You say You are. I have come into agreement with the lies of the devil. I have believed a lie concerning Your divine nature. Forgive me for allowing a perversion of Your Truth to direct my paths. I also realize that I have been involved in religious performance as I attempted to gain Your love and attention. Forgive me for not understanding the reasons for my actions and for not being sensitive to the times You desired intimacy.

Lord, I repent of the areas of [look over this chapter; wherever you marked, dog-eared or noted an area in which you know God is convicting you, take the time to repent for every action or sin].

Father, I believe Your Word, which states You are merciful and that it is Your desire to take me for Your inheritance. I repent of any involvement with idolatry and of the involvement of my ancestors. I lay the axe to the root of any sin and false belief systems.

Now, Lord, empower me with a spirit of Your might to be as Gideon and tear down every false image I may have.

I remain open to any other areas You might show me, concerning iniquitous patterns of behavior or belief systems. Thank You for forgiving me of my sins and the sins of my ancestors.

I declare that the enemy is not on the throne of my life. The one true God is the only one worthy of the throne, and I honor You, Lord.

In Jesus' mighty name, Amen.

Now rebuild an altar to the Lord through offering the sacrifice of praise. Spend some time reading through the Psalms, exalting His holy name and praising Him for who He is!

5

ATHALIAH'S REIGN
OF TERROR

Athaliah ruled the land.

2 Kings 11:3, NIV

Athaliah awoke early. After tossing and turning all night, it seemed the best thing was just to go ahead and get up. She made her way to her dressing table. Only a slight glimmer of sunlight brightened her handheld mirror.

"Oh, great! I can't even put on my color!" Athaliah scowled. Not the least bit concerned that she would awaken her handmaiden, she continued to complain. "Mother always knew how to look her best—even early in the morning. She could turn the head of any man on whom she set her sights. Except for that prophet guy. Well, I will just have to chance it and go out looking as though I just got out of bed. Maybe no one will notice me this early in the morning. I have too much on my mind to be all that concerned about how I look!"

Athaliah slowly and carefully made her way to the court-yard. Being extremely careful not to be seen, she opened the door to the courtroom quietly and stood for a moment, gazing at the king's throne. She began once more to recall that stupendous day when her husband was established as king of Judah. He had served on the throne for eight years, and now he was dead. Their son, Ahaziah, was now the king of Judah. "Oh, what I have accomplished! Just like my mother, Jezebel, I have influenced an entire nation. I brought my gods with me, and I have set them in every high place. I am highly favored by the gods as they are worshiped daily in the temples of Judah. Yes, all my gods are worshiped here; my husband was a king and I was a queen. But there is just one more thing—just one more dream left unfulfilled. . . . I want the throne!"

Athaliah wanted it all: the influence, the authority and the crown. Ruling from behind the throne gave her a degree of satisfaction, but not enough to satisfy her ambition to be in total authority over Judah. She had a spirit like a vulture, ready to encircle the weak and move in for the kill.

She had married a weak man, just as her mother had done. His name was King Jehoram of Judah. Like Ahab, Jehoram had also walked in the way of the kings of Israel. She had easily manipulated him to worship her gods in the same way her mother had convinced Ahab. As evil as her mother, Athaliah used every political platform to introduce Judah to Baal worship. She had high aspirations that her gods, Baal and Ashtoreth, would empower her to seize the crown and the throne.

Somehow I will find a way to sit in my son's place, she thought. *Just like my mother, I can do a much better job ruling and reigning. These weak men do not understand that it takes sheer determination and tenacity to govern a city! I could have conquered our enemies long ago if my husband and son had just listened to me. I have always had a better way. One day I will be able to prove myself to the courts.* Athaliah smiled as she began to scheme and fantasize about the day she would rule all Judah. "Ahaziah is now the king of Judah and just as much a fool as his father was. . . . I can handle him, too!" Athaliah was murmuring so loudly that one of the palace guards heard her.

"Your Majesty, are you calling for me?" The guard remained in the courtyard and waited for her to come to the door.

"No, be off with you! Can't a person be up early without someone taking notice?" Athaliah returned to her room and began to get ready. She could hardly get dressed due to her anticipation. She was going to be with her son later in the day and use her influence to make some needed changes. Whenever she spent time with her son, Athaliah had ulterior motives.

Later in the day, it was time to meet with the king. Athaliah had prepared and rehearsed her lists of "requests" to present to her son. She made her way toward the courts and started to open the courtroom doors.

"My lady! My lady! Come quickly!" A hysterical voice came down the long, narrow archway that led from the courtyard stairs.

Athaliah hurtled toward the voice. "What is it? What is wrong?"

"It is your son. It is the king! He is dead, my lady! He is dead!"

"What? What do you mean? What has happened to my son?" Athaliah was now running toward her son's lifeless body.

"Who? Who did this?" she demanded.

"The same man who destroyed Joram, king of Israel, has now killed Ahaziah, king of Judah. He is Jehu, the one the Hebrews call 'the anointed one.'"

"Jehu? You mean the same Jehu who destroyed my mother, my husband and the grandsons of the house of Ahab? Quick, we must take immediate action before this villain attempts to come here and seize the throne of Judah. Call forth the magistrates and the court officials; summon them immediately! Have them meet me in the king's court. Go, now . . . right now!"

Without allowing any time for mourning, she rushed to the king's court and sat on the throne. *Now!* she said to herself. *Now it is my turn! But first, I need to be sure that no one can overthrow my power. I have waited a lifetime to seize this position. I have only my grandsons standing in my way. I will deal with each of them in due time.*

Athaliah: The Destructive Seed of Jezebel

Athaliah was the generational seed of Jezebel and Ahab (see 2 Kings 8:18, 26). Some theologians believe she was their biological child and Omri's granddaughter. Others believe she was the daughter of Omri, and therefore the sister to Ahab, and that Ahab took her and became her father. The Hebrew word *daughter* used in 2 Kings 18:26 means "a daughter in the wide sense, and in terms of relationships, a branch, or company."

But whether Athaliah was a daughter or granddaughter, the full revelation of this translation represents a spiritual daughter—a daughter with the character or spirit—of Jezebel. If we translate *daughter* as "branch," then we gain a more correct understanding of Athaliah as a "branch" or "offshoot" from the "root" of Jezebel.

This would explain the evil atrocities Athaliah committed in murdering every male descendant to secure the throne of Judah. Just as Jezebel murdered God's anointed prophets, tried to kill Elijah and abort this mighty prophet's destiny, Athaliah destroyed the destiny of those called to rule and reign on the throne of Judah.

Athaliah was married to King Jehoram of Judah and became Judah's only queen in a rule that spanned from 841 to 835 B.C. (see 2 Kings 11:1–3 and 2 Chronicles 22, 23). She married a man who had the same characteristics as her father, Ahab. Not only did she follow in her mother's footsteps in choosing to marry a weak man, but she overthrew the legitimate heirs to the throne through manipulation and deception.

When her husband and son died, Athaliah illegally seized the throne as the absolute power in Judah. She then secured her future by murdering all her male descendants—yes, her grandsons! She destroyed anyone who threatened her power to rule over Judah. She had a hatred for legitimate and godly authority, going to extremes to destroy all opposition. Only the daughter of Jezebel could be so vicious and power hungry that she would murder her own grandsons to illegally seize the throne.

Like her mother, she was a murderer and an idolater who illegally seized dominion and authority. Jezebel introduced Israel to the idol Baal, and later her daughter, Athaliah, brought the same idols into Judah. Just as Jezebel seduced her husband into becoming an idol worshiper, Athaliah followed suit and encouraged hers to do the same. In the nation of Judah, therefore, not only was idol worship manifested, but also the release of the evil connected to each idol. The door to extreme oppression was now being opened in the land of Judah!

Dear ones, the same happens to us if we tolerate any manifestation of Jezebel and her seed.

Athaliah Targets the Generations

The spirits of Jezebel and Athaliah are almost identical in nature and deeds, so when we take authority over Athaliah, we can use the same prayer strategy we use against Jezebel. There are, however, two main differences.

First, Athaliah targets and attacks the generations of a family in order to ultimately destroy a people and a nation. Throughout history, leaders, mostly men, have targeted the destruction of generations. The Roman emperor Nero (who reigned from 54 to 68 A.D.), for example, murdered and persecuted thousands of Christians and then supposedly burned Rome. He was accused of murdering his own mother and wife, and possibly some of his advisors. Nero was extravagant, and he propagated belief in the Greek gods and the philosophy of humanism.

Another example is Adolf Hitler, who possessed the demonic ability to seduce the minds of an entire nation to elect him as leader of Germany, only then to rise to tyrannical and total dictatorial power. Once attaining that power, he legalized genocide in the countries he defeated and ruled. He murdered millions of Jews, as well as other "undesirables" such as the mentally retarded, minorities, etc. Through Hitler, Satan attempted to destroy all living Jews—the destruction of the generations—while aggressively seeking world domination.

Though the ambitions of Nero and Hitler varied, their underlying motive for power and dominion was the same. Obviously evil forces were working through these insane leaders, provoking them to perform these evil deeds.

Remember that the Jezebel spirit has no gender. This force will use both males and females to accomplish evil assignments upon the earth. Athaliah, as a woman, was possessed by the same spirits that later controlled Nero and Hitler. Just like her mother, Jezebel, she was determined to seize power any way she could and became determined to murder the generations after her in order to secure control.

The Spiritual Significance of Judah

Let's now look at the second difference between Jezebel and Athaliah. Because she was the queen of Judah, Athaliah directly targets all that Judah represents spiritually.

The territory of Judah, where Athaliah illegally reigned as queen, was the area named after Judah, one of the sons of Jacob and Leah. The property was the inheritance for the generations of Judah, a land for the tribe to possess and reign over with godly authority. Because it was dedicated to God, it was a place of praise to Him. But when Athaliah seized control, introduced her idols to the nation and then destroyed the legitimate heirs (the generations) to the throne, this area became defiled with idols and false worship.

So why did Satan, through Athaliah, want to destroy Judah? Genesis 49 reveals the prophetic significance of Judah. When Jacob, the father of the twelve sons who eventually became the twelve tribes of Israel, prophesied over each of his sons, he decreed a specific destiny over the descendants of each one. Unlike the prophecies over his other sons, Jacob went to greater length and detail for Judah. This is because out of the tribe of Judah David's throne would be established as a covenant promise. And later, Jesus, the King of Kings, would be born of David's lineage—the tribe of Judah.

Obviously, the need to preserve the destiny of this tribe was important for the future generations. It should be no surprise, then, that Athaliah desired to seize the throne and murder the generations. Through this destructive spirit, Satan was attempting to destroy the seed that would ultimately lead to King Jesus. Satan's ultimate goal was to destroy the lineage of our Savior!

Let's take a closer look at the prophecy and destiny of Judah, so we can better understand what Satan was attempting to destroy. In Genesis 49 Jacob gives his prophetic blessing:

> "Judah, you are he whom your brothers shall praise; your hand shall be on the neck of your enemies; your father's children shall bow down before you. Judah is a lion's whelp; from the prey, my son, you have gone up. He bows down, he

lies down as a lion; and as a lion, who shall rouse him? The scepter shall not depart from Judah, nor a lawgiver from between his feet, until Shiloh comes; and to Him shall be the obedience of the people. Binding his donkey to the vine, and his donkey's colt to the choice vine, he washed his garments in wine, and his clothes in the blood of grapes. His eyes are darker than wine, and his teeth whiter than milk."

Genesis 49:8–12

- Judah was prophesied to be one who was praised (verse 8).

  Judah is a Hebrew word that translates "praised." Praise is an act of worship. Through songs, worship, prayer or joyful expression, a true servant's heart praises our Lord for who He is and all He does (see Psalm 71:6, 14; 150:2; Matthew 25:21; 1 Corinthians 4:5; and Ephesians 1:3–14). Praise is God's weapon against the devil. No wonder Satan attacks the praisers!

- Judah's hand was to "be on the neck of [his] enemies" (verse 8).

  Judah is also translated as "to throw, shoot (arrows), cast, cast down, and to throw down." This refers to the warfare associated with Judah.

  The word *Judah* is also derived from a root word that refers to the "hand" and the strength and power of the hand. It is further linked with the strength in the hand and the portion of land. In other words, there seems to be a connection to Judah's strength to conquer, throw down and destroy by the strength in his hands. Plus, his strength lies in fulfilling destiny—that is, in possessing his inheritance.

Whenever God releases a prophetic destiny, our strength lies in possessing what God gives us. We are given the grace to fulfill destiny, and if we resign to having less, then we easily lose our strength and fulfillment. God promises to strengthen our hands to win the battle and possess our inheritance—for us and our future generations. King David, from the tribe of Judah, understood this principle as he praised God "who trains my hands for war, and my fingers for battle ... who subdues my people under me" (Psalm 144:1–2). Joshua, too, was from the tribe of Judah, and it was he who had a positive report concerning the Promised Land. The Lord therefore equipped Joshua to lead His people to cross over and possess the promise.

If Athaliah had had her way, however, neither David nor Joshua nor their descendants would have ever been born. The goal of this destructive stronghold was to abort the destiny of Judah and all its generations. After all, Satan was dealt his final blow by Jesus, the Lion from the Tribe of Judah!

Jesus would be the Lion of the Tribe of Judah who would rise up and destroy the enemy:

"The Lion of the tribe of Judah, the Root of David, has prevailed to open the scroll and to loose its seven seals."

Revelation 5:5

God always destined that One from the tribe of Judah would destroy the enemy. Athaliah would have loved to destroy every legitimate authority to the throne, including Jesus. Later, King Herod was obviously influenced by the demonic principalities of Athaliah and Jezebel. Yet another ruler who attempted to destroy the generations, he was informed that there was another "king" who was prophesied, and he ordered the murder of every male child in Bethlehem (see Matthew 2:16). Clearly the two demonic forces were once again working together to destroy the prophetic destiny of Christ and His descendants—us!

How many prophets and ruling spiritual kings are being aborted on a daily basis? We must pray for the Lord to empower us to defeat this evil anti-Christ stronghold that is destroying the generations.

God Preserves a Righteous Seed

In my recent book, *Destiny Thieves*, I document more thoroughly the evil manipulations of Athaliah in securing her illegal access to the throne of Judah. I should point out here, however, that one grandson escaped Athaliah's reign of terror. Athaliah's own daughter, Jehosheba, hid her nephew with the priesthood for six years in order to preserve the rightful heir to the throne.

Before Athaliah's seventh year as queen, the priesthood seized the opportunity to establish the prince into his rightful position and secretly aligned military forces to support him. In a secret temple ceremony, the child was crowned king. When Athaliah heard the people blowing trumpets and celebrating the ascension of Joash, the rightful heir, to the throne, she tore her clothes and yelled, "Treason!" (Jezebel and her seed will always falsely accuse others for what they themselves have done!) Athaliah was then taken from the Temple and executed in the streets. Jezebel's life ended in the streets, and so did her daughter's.

Thank God that He preserves a righteous seed—a remnant—to fulfill His perfect will! We always need to be praying for those seeds of righteousness to be divinely protected from the enemy's plans.

Defeating Goliath and Athaliah

Now let's look a little deeper into Athaliah's attack on Judah. As stated above, one of the definitions of *Judah* implies the action of casting and throwing, indicating conquest. David, even as a young man, understood the prophetic destiny he inherited as a descendant of Judah. He possessed the spiritual DNA to conquer his enemies, and he proved this first when he faced unafraid the feared giant Goliath. Inside of him was a determination not only to fulfill his destiny, but also to establish praise in a future tabernacle—all for the glory of God.

Remember how David carefully selected five smooth pebbles as his weapons? While the huge Philistine hurled intimidating threats, mocking David's age and size, the young boy remained focused for the battle. Without hesitation, he continued to gather five smooth stones for his sling. David knew he was a servant of the Most High God. He was a "praiser," and he knew how to give God all the glory. He might have been young, but he knew he was chosen.

This is what the enemy does to us as we select our weapons of warfare. We carefully plan, strategize and seek weapons of prayer strategy to defeat Athaliah, while the enemy hurls false accusations toward us, attempting to intimidate us. Listen to me: Keep praying! The devil has targeted our children, our seed, and the possession of our inheritance. If we listen to him, we will back off from the battle. David did not listen to Goliath. He kept focusing on the victory. We should do the same.

Why five stones? David must have believed that it might take all of them to defeat his enemy. He must have thought that if one or two did not do the trick, it would be prudent to have a few more. Also, Goliath had four brothers. In faith David could slay Goliath with the first stone; the other four were for the retaliating brothers! Similarly, we need several plans and prayers to overthrow our Goliaths. Being prepared with an arsenal of weapons is using wisdom.

Biblically, the number five represents grace, atonement, life, the cross and the fivefold ministries. But the number five also represents the five "I wills" of Satan. When Satan threatened to ascend above God's throne and His divine authority, he said "I will" five times (see Isaiah 14:13–14). So in choosing five stones, David was also overpowering the "I wills" of Goliath. These five "I wills" sounded like:

- "I will feed your flesh to the fowls of the air."
- "I will feed you to the beasts of the field."
- "I will certainly defeat you—all you have is a stick to war with!"
- "I will defeat you—you are too young to be a warrior."
- "I will utterly destroy you; no one that pretty could be a real man."

1 Samuel 17:41–44, paraphrased

As you gather your weapons of warfare, what five "I wills" is Satan hurling at you? Maybe he is speaking lies such as:

111

- "I will kill you."
- "I will destroy your marriage."
- "I will steal the lives of your children."
- "I will take all your possessions."
- "I will never allow you to be free."

Dear ones, the path to victory begins at the cross of Jesus. Realizing that He paid the price for your deliverance is the first step toward possessing every promise and defeating each Goliath.

Most of us know David's story and its ending. God honored the young man and his faith. After all, He is a God who honors faith, for without it we cannot please Him (see Hebrews 11:6). Even more, He is a covenant God who gave His Word that the tribe of Judah would rule and reign over its enemies. David was the one who just happened to believe it and do it.

David's destiny involved slaying Goliath, running from Saul, becoming king of all Israel, which included Judah, and planning a tabernacle of praise. But even more than this, Christ was born from David's lineage. The spirit motivating Athaliah to destroy her generations was also targeting the generations of David in order to destroy the line of Judah.

Athaliah's Attack upon David's Generations

Now let's take a look at Athaliah's planned assignments against David's generations. All parents love their children. And when our children do wrong, we suffer heartache. David was no different.

112

Six sons were born to David while he was in Hebron. In birth order they are Amnon, Chileab, Absalom, Adonijah, Shephatiah and Ithream (see 2 Samuel 3:2–5). Hebron represents a place of covenant. It was where Abraham built an altar as a sign of his covenant with God and God's covenant with him and his generations. Looking at Hebron prophetically, this was the place where God established covenant with David by blessing him with a generational seed that had the prophetic destiny to rule and reign forever over Judah. But the devil had a different plan.

Amnon raped his half sister Tamar and later was murdered by his brother Absalom. Amnon's name means "faithful" and is derived from a root word that means "to support, confirm, nourish, (to be) pillars, established and lasting (implying a lasting covenant)." The Lord gave David a son who established His covenant, yet Amnon chose to be the opposite of covenant. Instead, he was an incestuous rapist and a covenant breaker, unsupportive of his father. Instead of being a pillar in the house of God, Amnon rebelled against God's laws. How heartbreaking for David! His generations were being destroyed; Athaliah was on the prowl.

Chileab, David's second son, does not seem to have given David many problems—at least none that are documented. Maybe the devil skipped over one son to hurl his most fearsome blow against Absalom, for it was he who seems to have caused David the most grief.

Absalom was David's favorite. In Hebrew his name, *Abba shalom*, means "my father is peace." It is derived from another Hebrew word that means "prosperity, health, completeness, safety, soundness and contentment." Absalom was to be the fulfillment of God's covenant with David.

His name represents the Prince of Peace, Jesus, who came to give us eternal peace and was the fulfillment of our covenant with God. Yet Absalom was demonically influenced to choose another destiny. He murdered David's firstborn son, Amnon, betrayed David, raised his own army to defeat and destroy his father and then tried to take the throne. Absalom chose murder, betrayal, anger and rebellion as his destiny, and his choice ultimately led to his death. David was heartbroken. In Absalom we can identify the evil forces of Athaliah fully at work, for he plotted murder to illegally gain the throne of Judah.

Athaliah's plans did not stop with Absalom. After Absalom's death his younger brother Adonijah, David's fourth son, later rivaled Solomon for the throne.

Athaliah Thrives on Stealing the Destinies of Our Children

How many times have parents grieved over the paths their children have chosen? Jails are filled with God's children who have surrendered to the demonic powers of Athaliah and have chosen to murder, deceive, rob and remain in rebellion.

Precious ones, the devil targets our generations through the spirit of Athaliah. This demonic force does not surrender easily and seeks to destroy entire generations with only one person who will agree with her wicked plots for power.

Even Abraham Had to Fight for Lot!

If reading about Athaliah's attacks on David's sons is discouraging and makes you worry that it is impossible to

114

recover your generations, do not listen to the devil. Even Abraham went to war to save his nephew, Lot! Though Lot had chosen to live in Sodom, one of the "Twin Sin Cities," and expose his family to the degenerate lifestyles of its inhabitants, Abraham was empowered by the Lord to save his sinful family.

Lot and his family had been captured by four kings and had become slaves when Abraham came to the rescue. When he delivered Lot, Abraham was referred to as the "Hebrew," or "one who crosses over" (see Genesis 14:13). Abraham "crossed over" with a warfare mantle for his family.

We need to do the same. Abraham is our example of crossing over any rivers of doubt that God will save our families from death and despair.

The four kings Abraham battled reveal four warfare strategies that we can use for our families (see Genesis 14:9). By following the steps Abraham took to free his family from slavery, we can release our loved ones from demonic captivity.

- **The King of Elam: Chedorlaomer**

  His name implies a "binding up."

  The strategy of the spirit is to imprison by binding up with cords, or to bind so that one is unable to move forward. Many of our generations are in bondage with fear, doubt and "bent" mindsets. *Our strategy* is to ask the Holy Spirit to renew our minds, and then ask that He do the same for our future generations (see Romans 12:2; 2:16).

- **The King of Nations: Tidal**

  His name means "terrible, great fear, to make afraid," and to cause to "shrink back and crawl away." Another definition of the name *Tidal* is associated with the word *serpent*, which is another word for divination and witchcraft.

The strategy of the spirit is to cause such fear that we shrink back from warfare. *Our strategy* is to bind up occultic powers that hide truth and to advance forward in faith.

- **The King of Shinar: Amraphel**

  His name means "sayer of darkness."

  The strategy of the spirit is to speak darkness (doubt) over every situation. His words will never offer any hope. *Our strategy* is to speak words of faith and declare God's life over the death structures.

- **The King of Ellasar: Arioch**

  His name means "lion-like."

  The strategy of the spirit is to raise his head as a roaring lion that attempts to steal, kill and destroy. His is a false roar. *Our strategy* is to guard our ears and thoughts and not listen to the voice of the enemy.[5]

Standing in Faith for Your Generations

Out of the tribe of Judah came a power greater than Athaliah. His name is Jesus, the Lion of Judah. He is releasing a mighty roar over our generations. He is our covenant God, and we must begin to pray in faith, believing that our generations will fulfill the plan of God for their lives.

In His Word, God has given us several promises concerning our generations:

116

Promise #1: God promised to be our deliverer, even to our generations.

He said to Moses, "This is My name forever, and this is My memorial to all generations" (Exodus 3:15). God also said that He "would keep the oath which he had sworn unto your fathers, hath the LORD brought you out with a mighty hand, and redeemed you. . . . He is God, the faithful God, which keepeth covenant . . . to a thousand generations" (Deuteronomy 7:8–9, KJV).

Promise #2: We and our descendants can choose life.

God will remain faithful to all generations and have mercy upon them. He will establish your seed, and your descendants will live and not die (see Psalm 89:1–4). He said, "I have set before you life and death. . . . Choose life, that both you and your descendants may live" (Deuteronomy 30:19). He also said that "He remember[ed] His covenant . . . for a thousand generations" (Psalm 105:8) and that "His mercy is everlasting, and His truth endures to all generations" (Psalm 100:5).

Promise #3: God promised that our generations will always have a place in Him and enjoy His covenant promises.

The Lord said that He has been "our dwelling place in all generations" (Psalm 90:1). He also stated, "My righteousness will be forever, and My salvation from generation to generation" (Isaiah 51:8).

Do you see what is ours by birthright? The devil has no legal right to steal our seed!

Prayer for the Generations

Let's pray for our generations. I encourage you to pray the following prayer with me:

> Father, in the name of Jesus I stand upon Your Word, which declares that You will be a dwelling place for my generations. I decree that my generations will know You, serve You and dwell in Your house forever. You have said that Your righteousness will be forever and that Your salvation will endure from generation to generation. I decree that my generations will be righteous and will find their salvation in You. I ask that You send laborers forth for the salvation of my seed. I pray specifically for the salvation of [name those in your generations who need salvation]. I stand firmly upon my covenant promise from You. In Jesus' name.
>
> I believe Your Word, which states in Exodus 3:15 that Your name is forever and that You are the God of my generational seed. Lord, You have declared that You are the great *I Am*, the God of Abraham, Isaac and Jacob. You sent Moses to deliver Israel from the hand of Pharaoh. You have stated that You will be known throughout the generations as our God and Deliverer. I pray now for my generations [take some extra time to name the ones in your generation who need specific prayer], and I believe that according to Your Word You will deliver them from the destructive plans of the enemy. I stand upon Your Word, believing that You are not a God who lies but one who fulfills what You promise. You are the Redeemer of my generations. In Jesus' name.
>
> Lord, Your Word says that You are good and that Your truth and mercy endure to all generations. I thank You that You will remember the covenant that You made to the generations of Abraham. I am Abraham's seed—spiritual Israel—and I stand in faith believing that Your mercy and

truth are extended to my generations. I know that You are a covenant God and that Your Word is sure concerning my descendants. I pray specifically for [name your generations who need prayer]. I know that You show love and mercy, and I ask that You send ministering angels to minister life and truth to my generations. You have said that You will be faithful to the generations. I trust You, Lord, and I trust Your covenant promises to me.

In Jesus' name, Amen.

No sin is so great that God cannot forgive it. No river is so deep that He will not find us and save us from it. He is concerned for each of us and for our generations to come. His mercy endures forever!

Let's keep moving forward. In the next chapter are more specific prayer strategies to dethrone Jezebel and Athaliah and remove their evil influence from you and your generations.

6

PRAYING AGAINST THE DEMONIC POWERS OF JEZEBEL AND ATHALIAH

If my people, which are called by my name, shall humble themselves, and pray, and seek my face, and turn from their wicked ways; then will I hear from heaven, and will forgive their sin, and will heal their land.

2 Chronicles 7:14, KJV

God gives specific prayer strategies in His Word for battling the demonic powers of Jezebel and her seed, Athaliah. In

Revelation 2:18–29, He specifically addresses the church of Thyatira and rebukes this church for allowing the stronghold of Jezebel to seduce its members into tolerating her entanglements and influence. In verse 23 God says, "I will kill her children with death." Because Athaliah was as polluted as her mother, I believe that the prayer strategy given in Revelation is effective to overthrow the illegitimate authority of both of these seducing forces, Jezebel and Athaliah.

It is time to pull out your sword of the Spirit—God's Word—and use it against your enemies!

A Message for the Church Then and Now

In your Bible, quickly read Revelation 2 through 4, where the Lord addressed His churches—especially the church of Thyatira in Revelation 2:18–29. As you read, you will discover seven different messages to the seven different churches. Though these particular churches do not exist today, they represent the condition of the Church in the end times. Since we live in the end times, we need to observe carefully the teachings Christ gave to each of the churches. We are the Church. So not only is God speaking to the Church as a Body, but He also is speaking to the hearts of each of us! As we closely examine God's specific address to the church that tolerated Jezebel, we must allow Him to speak to our own hearts and receive His correction and instruction.

Are you ready? Have you read Revelation 2 through 4? Then let's proceed with open hearts to hear what the Lord has to say to us.

The Sevenfold Pattern

The Lord begins with the church of Ephesus (see Revelation 2:1). In His address to it and each subsequent church, He uses the same sevenfold pattern. In the Bible the number seven represents completion, so let's observe His pattern that leads us into destiny and total fulfillment.

Again, keep in mind that He was addressing the seven churches at that time, but the principles are just as relevant for each of us today. Allow the Lord to speak to your heart.

The sevenfold pattern is as follows:

- First, Christ gave a greeting to the particular church.

  For us today, it would be as if Christ were addressing our individual lives, churches or ministries and even calling us by name.

- Second, Christ designated Himself as the speaker and the One with the attributes to empower the church.

  For us today, it would be as if Christ were designating Himself as the Healer, Deliverer, Provider or any of His other many attributes. Depending upon the need of the assembly or individual, God designates Himself accordingly. If He were addressing a strong prophetic body of believers, for example, He might designate Himself as the Prophet or the Head of the Church and then reveal His will to perfect that body.

- Third, He commended, or praised, the church for what it was doing correctly.

  This would be the same for us today, as Christ might commend us for our diligence, service, faithfulness, etc.

123

- Fourth, He condemned, or rebuked, the church for the wrongs it had committed.

  For us today, Christ would address a certain situation in our lives or ministries and call for repentance and change.

- Fifth, Christ gave a warning in which He outlined the consequences the church faced if it remained on its present course.

  It is the same for us today. Christ directly points out and exposes our sin, explaining what will happen if we do not repent. His intent is always for us to turn from our wicked ways and totally commit to Him.

- Sixth, Christ gave an exhortation in which He instructed the church in how to set things right with Him and avoid judgment or destruction.

  This is when He applies discipline to correct what is wrong so that we are made whole and able to fulfill our destiny.

- And finally, Christ promised what He would do for the church that overcame the situation and embraced His Truth.

  This is when He exhorts us and encourages us to overcome. He further explains all the blessings and rewards that are attached to our obedience.

Part One: God Greets the Church of Thyatira

As I mentioned at the beginning of this chapter, the church of Thyatira was the church that allowed the entrance of the seductions of Jezebel, so this is where we will focus our study. God gave a divine pattern for prayer directives concerning those who tolerate Jezebel. And since Athaliah was Jezebel's seed, that force can be included in the divine prayer strategy. God begins His directive by greeting the church of Thyatira.

Let's first examine the city God is greeting. Thyatira was a city with no natural defenses. Because it was not built on a hill, it was subject to predators and military invasions. But even though its natural circumstances made the city vulnerable to its enemies, the inhabitants were an opposing foe of formidable strength. They were descendants of Macedonian soldiers and had retained much of their ancestors' military strength. Thyatira's other attributes were its strategic location and fertile soil. The Jews were attracted to the city because of its noted prosperity, especially in its commercial productivity with textiles and bronze armor.

Thyatira's commercial structure was part of the problem. It gives us insight into how the enemy infiltrates our churches today through Jezebel and Athaliah.

The city had established trade guilds, and the only avenue to becoming a successful businessman was to become a member of one of these organizations. The problem was that the members were forced to attend meetings/celebrations where idols were worshiped and the food was first sacrificed to the idols. If a Jew refused to attend the guild celebration, bow down to the idols or eat the food, he would lose his license of operation and be forced to shut down his business.

My father was a very successful businessman. On numerous occasions he achieved the "Salesman of the Year" award. During a season of climbing the corporate ladder to success, he felt pressure to join the Freemasons. He knew that those who were members of this organization promoted each other in business. I later found out that others in his business received promotions for belonging to this group. He ventured ahead and joined Freemasonry as an avenue to his success. His sales did not increase because of his new association; in fact, he later admitted that he felt more pressure to please others. He began to feel obligated to the "system" but was afraid to leave the organization because he had taken certain oaths of secrecy. Later, upon receiving knowledge of the demonic involvement associated with Freemasonry, my father repented and left the secret society.

✶ In Doris Wagner's excellent book on deliverance, *How to Minister Freedom*, the author exposes the curses attached to Freemasonry. She refers to "the evil eye" mentioned in Proverbs 28:22 as one of Satan's hidden snares: "A man with an evil eye hastens after riches, and does not consider that poverty will come upon him." The author points out that the spirit behind the occult causes truths to become hidden and concealed. Satan is crafty in his techniques of warfare, and if he can conceal truth, then he can deceive us. Those with an "evil eye" are deceived by powers of darkness and blinded to the light (truth). Freemasonry is full of massive deception and uses the evil eye to influence its members. While many who are involved in Freemasonry believe that it promotes morality, brotherhood and a godly lifestyle, it is, in fact, a false religion. For those of you who have been involved with Freemasonry or have family members who have, I strongly suggest that you submit to someone for further deliverance.

126

I also highly recommend Doris Wagner's book, as well as Dr. Selwyn Steven's *Unmasking Freemasonry: Removing the Hoodwink* (www.jubilee-resources.com).

My father's belief that success was connected to Freemasonry was not an isolated one. Such organizations are entrenched in many cities, and business owners are pressured into joining these associations to remain in business. The Lord rejects submission to these types of secret societies, especially if the motivation is for success and money. We must not attempt to control our own future success: "Then you say in your heart, 'My power and the might of my hand have gained me this wealth.' And you shall remember the Lord your God, for it is He who gives you power to get wealth, that He may establish His covenant which He swore to your fathers, as it is this day" (Deuteronomy 8:17–18). The Lord is the only one who actually gives wealth. Forgetting who gives wealth is idolatry, and the result could be death: "And it shall be, if thou do at all forget the Lord thy God, and walk after other gods, and serve them, and worship them, I testify against you this day that ye shall surely perish" (verse 19, kjv). We cannot bow to trade guilds, unions or organizations that do not exalt our Lord. Do not be afraid or intimidated to do what is righteous in the eyes of the Lord!

Success is often viewed through deceptive lenses. Churches are viewed as successful only because of large numbers and mammoth-sized buildings. Businessmen and women are deemed successful if what they "do" works. But to God, success is not about money or fame. God says, "Remember My teachings and instructions and obey them completely. . . . Let love and loyalty always show . . . and write them in your mind. . . . God and people will like you and consider you a success" (see Proverbs 3:1–5). True success is the fruit of godly obedience.

The spirit of mammon promotes the love of money, which is the root of evil (see 1 Timothy 6:10). (We will discuss the spirit of mammon in greater detail later when we look at the spirit of Delilah in chapter 7.) The love of money can become an idol to which we bow down. Don't be deceived as the church of Thyatira was!

I must point out that though Thyatira was drenched in idolatry and the businessmen submitted to the control of the guilds, the city boasts its first Christian convert: Lydia, the seller of purple. This is an encouragement to Christian businesspeople; believers do not have to bow down to Jezebel in order to be successful! The destructive force of Jezebel will attack finances, but God will bring increase when His people stand up to the controlling, demonic forces of Jezebel.

Part Two: God Reveals His Attributes

I get excited when I reveal to others this part of the sevenfold pattern. God actually tells us how to address Him, what attributes to call upon and which name to use when we battle the Jezebel stronghold.

In the Old Testament, God revealed Himself in different ways to His people, and He gave Himself various names to identify His omnipotent attributes. He revealed Himself, for example, as *Jehovah Rapha*, "God Our Healer." He does the same thing in His pattern for the seven churches. When

He addresses each church, He also explains how to address Him in the attributes needed for the situation.

In the letter to Thyatira God addresses Himself as "the Son of God, who hath his eyes like unto a flame of fire, and his feet are like fine brass" (Revelation 2:18, KJV). He is exalting His divine position as the Lord and stating the fact that no other (false) god can stand before Him.

Even more specifically, God is directly opposing the man-made strength of the trade guilds that fashioned bronze armor (in which the people of the city took great pride!) and monetary coins. The coins portrayed a false god—a coppersmith, the god Hephaestus—hammering a helmet on an anvil. In creating such a coin, the smiths of Thyatira were recognizing Hephaestus as the creator who blessed financially. The Lord is opposing and condemning this practice and identifying Himself as the only God of prosperity. He is stating that He is the only one who creates the flame and acknowledging that His feet are of the finest brass, which man cannot duplicate.

Today there is much compromise in the business sector. Some easily toss morality aside to gain wealth. The movie industry is merely one of the avenues of immorality. The love of money is the primary motive for multitudes of businesses. Although money is necessary, as Christians we cannot bow down to compromise. The people of Thyatira had committed fornication (followed other gods) and eaten foods sacrificed to idols, and when we bow down to compromise and immorality in order to achieve worldly success, we are guilty of the same sins they were. Bowing down to an ungodly culture only opens doors to future despair. We must begin to focus on eternity and dedicate our money, businesses and lifestyles to God.

On a personal level, God is also addressing sins of compromise, such as eating and digesting the words of the enemy and believing Satan's lies over God's words. Have we given a place to Jezebel? We do so any time we compromise morality for money and success.

God identified Himself as the "Son of God, who hath his eyes like unto a flame of fire, and his feet are like fine brass" (verse 18, KJV). His eyes have already seen our sin. But His fire can purify us, cleanse us and direct our paths. If we have given any place to the spirit of Jezebel, we can position ourselves at His feet of fine brass and be purified. If we have fallen away, we can quickly repent of our sin, embrace His fire and become fully restored and forgiven.

Furthermore, Christ is stating that He is His Word, and His Word will stand sure and steadfast. He is the judge over the city. Man-made idols are no match for the One with the feet of fine brass, a substance against which the idols will not be able to stand or compete. Simply stated, if we recognize the power of His Word and submit to His Word as well as His purification and holiness, we will receive life. Life can come only through Christ; therefore, by tolerating Jezebel and her seed, Athaliah, we are opening doors to death structures.

God's eyes of fire and feet of brass will overthrow our enemy!

Part Three: Christ's Commendation

The next part of the pattern is Christ's commendation to the saints at Thyatira for their love, faith, service and endurance. Without love, the Word states that we are simply making a lot of noise! We can prophesy, sing songs and make joyous worship, but if we do not have love, then God is not pleased (see 1 Corinthians 13:1–4, 8, 13).

In our role as pastors, when we have corrected someone who entertained a Jezebel influence, we tried to operate in love. We knew that the person was responding out of a deep spirit of rejection. For us not to love the person would be setting him or her up for failure, so we tried our best to walk in love. We would have no mercy, on the other hand, on this spirit of darkness, and we would not allow our positions of authority to be compromised.

Notice once more that Jesus commended Thyatira for its love, faith, service and endurance. Jezebel will go full force after faith-based ministries and churches that are alive, serving the community and enduring hardships because the spirit knows how powerful the Word of God is. This is why we must recognize Jesus and His Word, praying the Word and allowing the cleansing of the Word to wash over the situation.

Part Four: Christ's Condemnation

Though Thyatira was doing well in love, faith, service and endurance, the church was rebuked for tolerating the heretical teachings of Jezebel and her paganism. As I have previously stated, godly correction is needed. Those whom Christ loves He also chastises (see Hebrews 12:5–7).

Some believe that Christ does not rebuke or condemn. The Word does say that "there is therefore now no condemnation to them which are in Christ Jesus," but it goes on further to say, "who walk not after the flesh, but after the Spirit" (Romans 8:1, KJV). This passage is clear that there is condemnation for those who are not walking after the Spirit and are guided by the flesh. Because the church of Thyatira was led by the flesh and a demonic spirit, it suffered Christ's condemnation.

Let me remind you that Jezebel called herself a prophetess, which she was not, and then taught and seduced the people to commit fornication and eat foods sacrificed to idols. I have already discussed how the enemy can falsely prophesy, and if we believe what he says, then God considers this idolatry. It is the same as eating foods sacrificed to idols; in essence, we are eating the devil's words. So we see how Jezebel operated here.

But what about the fornication? During the trade guild festivals, people not only consumed the foods sacrificed to idols, but they also participated in licentious rites in which religion and sex were mingled. So in addition to consuming the devil's portion, the young church at Thyatira had been seduced to embrace lawlessness, superstition, devil worship, legalism and sexual sin. They had become especially vulnerable to false doctrine if the teachings were catering to the "lusts of the flesh."

But we must not limit the fornication and idolatry to these examples. Another example is embracing a spirit of whoredoms. If we open our lives to the spirit of whoredoms, then we also open the door to a Jezebel stronghold.

The spirit of whoredoms is noted in Hosea 5:4: "They will not frame their doings to turn unto their God: for the spirit of whoredoms is in the midst of them, and they have not known the LORD" (KJV). The spirit of whoredoms manifests in several different ways:

- Unfaithfulness/adultery
- Spirit, soul or body prostitution
- Chronic dissatisfaction
- Love of money
- Fornication
- Idolatry
- Excessive appetite
- Worldliness

Most Westerners today do not bow down to physical idols. But whatever comes between us and our relationship with the Lord is considered by Him to be an idol. If you notice any of these manifestations operating in your life, you may be influenced negatively by the spirit of Jezebel.

What rules your life? Is it your job? Your money? Your children? Does pleasure have first place? How about food, sex, sports or television?

Even religion, if it supersedes our relationship with Christ, can be an idol. The enemy is sly. If he cannot seduce us into immorality, he entices us with religion and legalism. We must remember that we do not have allegiance to a church; we have allegiance to Christ. Our first loyalty is to Him. We are to be God-pleasers, not man-pleasers. We are to be committed not to "dead works" but to the living God.

Whatever dominates us has first place in our lives, and the Lord considers it idolatry. We are instructed to keep our eyes upon Jesus and behold only Him.

The Word says, "The just shall live by faith" (Romans 1:17, KJV). Faith is one of the godly attributes that defeats the seductive enticements of the Jezebel spirit. Our faith must be in God and His ability to feed, nourish and care for us. Trusting in money, other relationships or other activities is idolatry. By trusting in His ability to care for us, we lift Jesus higher, and that always defeats the enemy. This is the way we tear down the enemy from his high place.

Part Five: Christ's Warning

Christ warned Thyatira that if it did not repent of its evil deeds, it would face certain consequences. The root of its sin was tolerating Jezebel. Jesus said He would "cast [Jezebel] into a sickbed, and those who commit adultery with her" (Revelation 2:22). This means her followers would become open prey to sickness and disease, as well as to demons associated with the spirit of whoredoms. Similarly, if we tolerate Jezebel today, then our sin could open doors to death assignments, generational curses of infirmity and premature death.

Jesus also said Jezebel's followers would suffer great tribulation unless they repented (see Revelation 2:22). *Tribulation* is defined as "tremendous pressure, affliction and great distress." If we continue to tolerate Jezebel and do not repent, then we, too, will suffer tribulation.

Finally, Jesus warned that Jezebel's children would be killed (see Revelation 2:23). This represents a death assignment against the seed of her followers—both natural and spiritual children. A death assignment is attached to Jezebel and the threefold cord. Remember: Athaliah destroyed her seed. If these spirits are tolerated, the enemy has an open door to destroy your seed, which includes both natural and spiritual pregnancies.

134

Part Six: Christ's Exhortation

Isn't it wonderful that Christ exhorts us? He so loves us and is forever encouraging us to repent so that we may experience forgiveness.

Christ exhorted Thyatira to repent, and He exhorted those who had not followed the teachings of Jezebel. He told these others to "hold tightly to what you have until I come" (Revelation 2:25, NLT).

It seems a simple statement: "Hold tightly to what you have." But we also know how crafty Satan is! It is my full-time job just to "hold on"! I would surmise that the pressure in Thyatira was tremendous against those trying to "hold on." Even Adam and Eve, who walked with God, could not hold on to their authority and were easily seduced into believing a lie. It is a battle to hold on to faith, finances, one's relationship with God and one's future. Be careful! Though you may feel you have not allowed Jezebel to influence your life, this evil spirit is waiting for a prime opportunity to seduce you into sin. Be sober and vigilant, and you will win the battle.

Part Seven: Christ's Reward

Christ promises a reward to all who overcome the Jezebel influence:

> "And he who overcomes, and keeps My works until the end, to him I will give power over the nations—'He shall rule them with a rod of iron; they shall be dashed to pieces like the potter's vessels'—as I also have received from My Father; and I will give him the morning star."
>
> Revelation 2:26–28

First, those who overcome will receive authority over all the nations; they will rule with an iron rod and smash them like clay pots. Psalm 2:9 mentions the same authority that is given to Christ. In Revelation 2:26 He makes it clear He is giving that authority to every believer who refuses to succumb to the wiles of Jezebel.

He also says we will receive the "morning star," which is the light that shines in the midst of darkness. Morning Star is another name for Christ (see Revelation 22:16). He is the fountain of all light and the morning light of prophecy and prophetic fulfillment. He assures us of the light of a day of fulfillment approaching. He is our source of hope and fulfilled promise.

Note that He gives us a rod of iron if we overcome. Precious saints, God is going to give us His iron scepter to defeat the spirits of Jezebel and her seed. By giving us His scepter, He empowers us with greater measures of authority to defeat our enemies. Jesus has already overcome the world, and now He is giving us that same authority. He knows that the enemy desires to dominate us. The word *dominate* means "domain." The devil desires to take our inheritance, our domain. But God gives us all power and all authority over the wicked one. Saints, we must rise up and exercise our authority over the devil. The Word says to submit to God, resist the devil and he will flee. Rise up and resist so that you may rule and reign!

You may be asking, "What am I supposed to be overcoming?" The answer is, any area of your life you do not dominate. Wherever the enemy has dominion in a person's life, he or she is enslaved. If you are a slave to lust and perversion, overcome with purity and love. If you are a slave to lies and dishonesty, then overcome with truth. If you are a slave to impure thoughts and motives, overcome with God's ability to renew your mind. These are simple examples of overcoming the enemy through spiritual warfare.

The Word of God says to "choose life." One of the greatest weapons we have is the ability to make right choices. If we choose what is right in God's eyes, He gives us the grace and power to accomplish that choice. By choosing life, we can defeat every death structure the enemy has planned against us. Choose today not to tolerate Jezebel her daughter any longer!

How to Pray to Overcome Jezebel

The sevenfold pattern of Christ's instructions to the church of Thyatira provides divine direction in prayer to overcome Jezebel:

- First, thank God that He is who He says He is (how He describes Himself).
- Thank Him for the good that He notices concerning the situation.
- Pray a prayer of repentance concerning the areas He rebukes.
- Thank Him for the reward and ask Him to strengthen you to overcome the enemy.

Below is a simple guideline that follows Christ's prayer directive concerning Jezebel. Keep in mind that as you pray, you are dethroning the power of Satan through repentance. Remember that every idol (false belief system, "bent" attitude, idolatry) must be torn down so that the enemy is dethroned. Since we prayed in previous chapters to dethrone the spirits that operate with Jezebel's false gods, especially Baal and Ashtoreth, then Athaliah will have no legal right to remain either. Finally, we will praise the Lord for who He is and rebuild an altar to Him, thus establishing His truth. When you pray, remain focused, but please do not become legalistic and get stuck in a "set form" of prayer. Allow the Holy Spirit to lead you in directing your prayers.

Part One of Prayer: Addressing His Divine Attributes (See Revelation 2:18)

Lord Jesus, I thank You that You are the Son of God, the One who has eyes like flames of fire and feet of brass. I praise You because Your eyes see all things. You are able to see the beginning and the end, and You are the Alpha and Omega. Lord, You are able to see my future, and I ask that You guide me through this battle opposing the seducing spirits of Jezebel and Athaliah. I ask for Your supernatural impartation of spiritual discernment and an ability to see how to go into battle. Since You see all things hidden, I ask You to reveal what is hidden so that I can do warfare with confidence. I ask You to burn away all iniquity within my life so I can be a pure vessel. As I confront the Jezebel influence, I pray that Your fire would purge and cleanse all my thoughts, deeds and motives. I thank You for igniting my faith with a Holy Spirit fire. I position myself at the feet of Christ, fully submitting my life, my finances, my family and [name other areas on

138

your heart] to You. I repent of my selfish ambitions, self-gratification and self-justification and my desires to please man more than You. I repent also of all idolatry, lusts of the flesh and areas of rebellion. Today I am determined to be a God-pleaser, and I pray that Your Holy Spirit will lead me into all truth.

Part Two of Prayer: Affirming His Commendations (See Revelation 2:19)

Though You have said I have a measure of faith and love, I ask that You increase my faith and empower me to walk in love. Conform me into Your image so I can reflect Christ Jesus, the Anointed One, on this earth. I desire to continue in my commitment and service to You, Lord. As I continue to run the race, empower me to endure all things that may challenge my faith so I can be a testimony to Your glory.

Part Three of Prayer: Repenting for Sins That He Condemns (See Revelation 2:20–24)

I repent of partaking of any form of idolatry, agreeing with the lies of Satan and [name any other areas on your heart]. I ask that You save me from all tribulation, deliver me from the spirit of infirmity, death and any death structure that the enemy attempts to erect around my family, business or ministry. I rebuke every spirit of Athaliah that kills the godly seed, seduces and defiles. I loose the power of the Most High God, the Alpha and Omega, into every situation that concerns me. [As the Holy Spirit directs, allow Him to take you through any area of repentance that is necessary; take time on this section.]

Part Four of Prayer: His Exhortation (See Revelation 2:24–25)

Now, Lord, I ask that You empower me to hold fast to what I have. I believe that Your divine strength will sustain me and that You give Your angels charge over me. The angels will not allow me to stumble or fall, and You will continue to watch over me.

Part Five of Prayer: Confessing Your Reward for Overcoming Jezebel and Athaliah (See Revelation 2:26–29)

I thank You, Lord, that I will overcome and will receive power to rule over the nations. With Your scepter of iron, I will crush the enemy and all plans of destruction. I will overpower every Jezebel assignment that comes against me, my family or my ministry [you may need to name individuals, churches, ministries, etc.]. As You promised, I declare that the enemy's plans are crushed like pottery into tiny pieces. I decree that I am an overcomer and that I am empowered to defeat the enemy. I am thankful for Jesus, my Morning Star, who shines brightly into my future and empowers me with great faith and hope. I decree that my ears hear what the Spirit of the Lord says to me.

In Jesus' mighty name, Amen.

Now stand up and give the Lord a mighty shout of victory! Hallelujah!

In Conclusion

The example I have given as a prayer strategy against Jezebel can also be used against her seed. Again, do not limit all your prayers to this one form. Most likely, the Lord will expand your understanding and strategy. But God has provided His divine pattern for overcoming Jezebel. As we pray we must heed His direction, and the prayer I have outlined does that.

My prayer for you is that now you are more fully equipped to dethrone the powers of darkness attempting to rob you of your future.

Pray with faith against the threefold cord. Repent of sin and then rebuild an altar to God. Aggressively agree with His Word and His promises. You will become transformed into His image!

7

THE EVIL POWER
OF DELILAH

And it came to pass afterward, that he loved a woman in
the valley of Sorek, whose name was Delilah.

Judges 16:4, KJV

In chapter 1 we learned of the threefold cord attacking the
Church. We have studied two of the most powerfully seducing strongholds named in the Bible. The last to expose
is the spirit of Delilah.

Delilah is the third part of the threefold cord that tries
to build death structures over us. Remember that death
structures are built upon the past, and the purpose of this
book is to expose and overthrow the demonic powers that

attempt to lock us into the past. This is the season to make the past submit to the future.

Once again, get that pen or marker ready and feel free to underline or highlight any area the Holy Spirit illuminates. As you read further, you may discover a particular pattern of behavior from which the Lord desires to deliver you. Or He may expose generational tendencies that have opened the door for seducing spirits to attack you. Whenever the Lord reveals an area where He desires to minister to you, be accountable to Him and document (underline, highlight or journal) what He reveals. At the end of this chapter is another strategic opportunity to be set free from powers of darkness that attempt to steal future breakthroughs and victories.

Ready? Let's move forward and allow the Spirit of the Lord to reveal new truths that will expose the maneuvers of the enemy so that we are loosed from his planned captivities.

The Story of Samson

Samson was from the tribe of Dan. Like the other Israelites, the Danites never conquered all their allotted territory, losing all but the regions of Zorah and Eshtaol to the Philistines and the Amorites. At the time, the Philistines had dominion over Israel. This tribe also was strongly rooted in Baal and Dagon worship. (We will discuss Dagon more fully in the next chapter.)

Samson's family was from Zorah. His mother was barren, but the angel of the Lord appeared to her and promised her a son who was to be raised a Nazirite. The Lord gave her specific instructions regarding the raising of Samson and declared that "he [would] begin to deliver Israel out of the hand of the Philistines" (Judges 13:5).

Both of Samson's parents were fully committed to God and were pleased to dedicate their son to Him. They raised Samson according to the divine instructions of the Lord: no razor touched his head, he was not allowed strong drink or wine and he did not eat any unclean thing. Samson became the hope of Israel. He single-handedly slew thousands of the Philistines and destroyed their crops. When the Spirit of the Lord came upon him, Samson became supernaturally empowered to slay the enemies of Israel. Samson, however, had a weakness, and that weakness was women—the wrong women. His first love was a daughter of the Philistines, who at that time had dominion over Israel. Samson's parents urged Samson to marry among his own people, but Samson said, "She pleaseth me well" (Judges 14:3, KJV). Samson's eyes deceived his spirit. He married her but was later betrayed by her and the Philistines.

Samson then became entangled with a harlot, and the Philistines found him and sought to entrap him. His ungodly relationships led him down pathways of heartache and destruction and made him vulnerable to the seductions of evil. One might reason that he would run quickly in the opposite direction, away from another Philistine woman, but the seductive powers of the defiling stronghold entwined him until his defeat.

When Samson found Delilah, he seemed to have lost all sense of responsibility. Fulfilling his God-ordained destiny to defeat Israel's enemies took a backseat to the seductions of Delilah. Once more Samson crossed a boundary and defiled his vow to God.

Delilah, the "Delicate One"—Yeah, Right!

Besides Jezebel, Delilah is probably the most evil seducer of God's anointed. Delilah lived close to where Jezebel was born, so she was prey to the same spirits and seductive tendencies as Jezebel and Athaliah. The difference was that Delilah was not a murderer; she was motivated by the love of money and the spirit of mammon.

It was easy, then, for the Philistines to hire Delilah to betray and destroy Samson. When Samson rose in power, he was a threat to every tribe and nation. To protect their regions and military strength, five Philistine kings offered Delilah a bribe if she would conspire with them to bring Samson to his knees. As Samson's mistress, her assignment was to discover the secret of his enormous strength and then to weaken that strength.

Judges 16:5 describes the strategy of the Philistines:

> *Entice* him, and *see wherein his great strength lieth*, and by what means we may *prevail* against him, that we may *bind him* to *afflict him*; and we will give thee every one of us eleven hundred pieces of silver.
>
> Judges 16:5, KJV, emphasis mine

Delilah was being hired to:

- "Entice" Samson. *Entice* means "to lead on by exciting hope or desire, to allure and to tempt."
- "See wherein his great strength lieth." She was to examine his strength so the kings could target and destroy that strength.

146

- Find out how the kings could "prevail against him." *Prevail* means "to prove superior in strength and power."
- "Bind him." One of the definitions of *bind* is "to imprison."
- "Afflict him." *Afflict* translates as "to oppress, humble, be afflicted, and be bowed down."

Delilah manipulated Samson until she got her answer. God had promised to give Samson strength only if he kept the Nazirite vow. When Delilah learned this, she cut his hair while he was sleeping, and his strength left. The Philistines then bound him and put out his eyes. He was taken into Gaza, the city of the Philistine giants, totally humiliated and ashamed. The strong man who had slain thousands of his enemies was now their slave, bound in chains and grinding grain in the prison house. (Talk about a lockdown!) Thus, a man anointed with God's might was seduced by a woman employed by idol worshipers and was reduced to a lowly slave.

Interestingly, Delilah's name is translated as "delicate," but its root meaning is "to be brought low, to hang down and to be languid." *Languid* means "slow, lifeless, fatigued, weak, lacking in spirit and listless." As her name indicates, Delilah brought Samson low and weakened him.

Satan sent Delilah to steal the strength of Samson. He chose one who appeared outwardly to be "delicate" but who had a heart filled with evil intentions. She was pleasing to the eye—maybe even fragile and dainty. Her evil intentions, however, were manipulation and seduction—adequate weapons to drain the very life from the strongest man of

God. Samson, who was seduced by her "delicacies," was at one time a spiritual Hercules, courageous and larger than life in action and deed. Yet in the clutches of Delilah, he was reduced to weakness, slowness and lifelessness. He was brought down and made low in the sight of all who observed his decline.

Delilah perverted Samson's passion. She seduced him and then perverted and redirected his passion. He turned his passion away from God and focused it instead on worldly pleasures. Through her seductions, Delilah destroyed Samson's destiny.

Satan has targeted each of us with the same intentions. He employs seducing spirits to steal the lives and destinies of God's strong warriors. He perverts our passion and redirects it toward worldly pleasures. We can, however, be well fortified and remain on guard against his seductions by observing the evil maneuvers of Delilah.

The Five Philistine Kings Who "Bought" Delilah

I want to offer a more in-depth look at the Philistine kings who were the power behind Delilah's actions (see Joshua 13:3). These five kings were no dummies. Though Samson was physically strong, they knew his weakness. They searched for a woman who could be enticed and bought with money. They found Delilah, a woman with no conscience and who coveted money more than morality. They knew they could use her to trample down Samson and weaken him so that all Israel would remain oppressed.

The translation for *Philistine* is "to wallow in the mud." The Philistine stronghold is an unclean spirit that seeks to defile all it touches. By carefully studying each of these kings, we gain strategies to defend ourselves against the spirits seeking to defile us and rob us of our strength, tenacity and destiny.

Below are the names of the five kings, followed by the meanings of their names. As you read through them, remember to note any area where you may be vulnerable to Satan's plans of destruction or where you might easily be seduced. At the end of the chapter we will fortify our strengths and be empowered to further defeat our enemy.

The Lord of the Gazathites

This king was from Gaza. When Moses allotted the twelve tribes of Israel their inheritance, Gaza was to have been destroyed by Joshua. But Joshua was unable to do so. Judah finally overtook the land but eventually lost control, and the Philistines regained Gaza. Samson was called to take back this territory for Israel, but he was unable to fulfill his destiny because of the wiles of Delilah. Gaza therefore remained the possession of the Philistines, who worshiped their false god, Dagon. The city was doomed by the prophets (see Jeremiah 47:1, 5; Amos 1:6–7).

In Hebrew, *Gaza* means "fortified and strong." The plans of this unclean stronghold are fortified and strong in its actions against us. The enemy seeks to establish a well-fortified place in our lives to establish a "strong hold." I am reminded of what my mentor and father in the Lord, Bishop Bill Hamon, preaches. He says a strength left unguarded is a double weakness. By this he means that if we feel we are well-fortified in a particular area but do not protect it, then the enemy easily can move right in, and soon our strength becomes a double weakness. I knew a pastor, for instance, who said his marriage could never be attacked. He wrote books on how to have successful, godly marriages, and he sponsored marriage seminars. Then credible prophets warned him of an attack by the devil concerning his marriage. He boasted with pride that it was impossible for Satan to penetrate this area. Within three months the pastor had an adulterous affair with the church secretary. It was a sad situation. His marriage was destroyed, and five children were devastated. And, of course, his church body suffered from the destruction, as well.

Each of us has strength, but Delilah plans to steal it! Be on guard against her evil seductions. To think that we are spiritually impenetrable and immune to Satan's seductions is like wearing a bull's-eye, daring Satan to shoot fiery darts and hit the mark. On the other hand, we can use the strength God has given us, submit it to Him and possess our Promised Land. Let's be focused and firmly fixed on every promise God has given and use it as strength to rise up and defeat the devil. Unlike Joshua and the Israelites who stopped short of their victory in Gaza, let's not quit until we have taken the land and put the enemy under our feet!

The Lord of the Ashdothites

This king was from Ashdod. Judah seized control of this land, but the Philistines regained power over it. Ashdod also was doomed by the prophets (see Isaiah 20:1; Jeremiah 25:20).

150

The name *Ashdod* means "a fortified place," and *Ash-dothite* means "to oppress and act violently." The names further translate as "divided rock, to divide, cut up." From these translations we understand that the enemy seeks to divide us. This unclean spirit causes church splits by bringing disputes and divisions in the Body of Christ, especially in doctrine. The evil spirit is strategically positioned against the Church and attempts to oppress every believer to rob him or her of faith and vision. But God promises to equip and empower us to gain victory over the strategies of the enemy.

One might think that detecting this type of spirit would be easy. But then why are there so many church splits and divisions over doctrine, and why is there so much disharmony in the Body of Christ?

In God's Church, Satan seeks one whom he can seduce to be his weapon; that is, he first finds a Delilah who will submit to his strategies of strife, division and rebellion. Then he uses that Delilah to seduce Samson.

Satan Uses Power and Mammon to Seduce Delilah to Action

Satan approached Delilah with a vision of power by offering her wealth to seduce Samson and secure the Philistines' victory. Can't you imagine the visions of grandeur she had? She sold out to the devil for a vision of more things. Many times today Satan finds his willing Delilahs with the same seduction of power and recognition. These "power plays" often lead to church splits.

Money is neutral; it is neither good nor bad. It is simply a means of exchange. The love of money, however, is what causes trouble. The love of money invites the spirit of mammon, which influences people to sell out to the lusts of the flesh. This stronghold truly gains a "strong hold" on our desires.

I have observed families who have received financial inheritances that were meant to be blessings. The blessings, however, seemed to become curses! The family members allowed greed to manifest, and a spirit of mammon began to cause strife and division among them. In such instances, the inheritance was not the problem; the love of money became the problem. When a spirit of mammon is present, people begin to "look out for number one." When this evil influence is active, family members who were once close become enemies as their inheritance is divided.

Looking out for number one is not a Kingdom mentality; it is an attitude of building one's own kingdom. The spirit of mammon focuses on selfishness with no thought to building the Kingdom of God. Kingdom finances, for example, are not to be used solely to build large church buildings that exhort fleshly desires for power.

God does not release wealth so that we look successful and our egos are exhorted. Money and wealth are given to us by God to build His Kingdom and attain His purposes upon the earth; therefore, the Kingdom finances are not for us individually.

"Then you say in your heart, 'My power and the might of my hand have gained me this wealth.' And you shall remember the LORD your God, for it is He who gives you power to get wealth, that He may establish His covenant which He swore to your fathers, as it is this day."

Deuteronomy 8:17–18

Referring to money and mammon, Jesus said that we could not serve two masters (see Matthew 6:24). He meant that mammon could become a master over us. If we are not careful, each of us could easily become a slave to a spirit of mammon. We could be seduced to exchange our godly inheritance for self-satisfaction and worldly pleasures. The enemy would love for us to sell our birthrights! We must not let him use any of us as a Delilah.

God does, of course, desire to bless us, and He states so in His Word. We are to seek first the Kingdom of God, and then all things will be given to us (see Matthew 6:33).

It is time to examine our hearts concerning money versus mammon and be committed to building His Kingdom and not our own.

Take note of the following characteristics of the spirit of mammon:

- Constant worry and anxiety over money
- Poor money management (spending more than you have because you need to feel good about yourself or appear successful to others)
- Consistent financial lack
- Having a poverty mentality (consistently confessing, "I can't afford it")
- Impulse buying (wanting things *now*)
- Selfishness and self-centeredness
- Greed and covetousness

- Chronic dissatisfaction (no matter how much you have, it is never enough)
- Bondage of debt
- Exaggerated estimation of money and power

The Lord of the Eshkalonites

Okay, back to the kings! This third king was from Askelon, a territory that belonged to Judah but was retaken by the Philistines. It remained a Philistine city that fought against both Judah and Israel many times.

Are you beginning to see the pattern here? Once more Judah had possession of the inheritance, and the Philistines took it back! The territory once possessed by God's chosen was stolen by the enemy—over and over and over again. How long was Israel going to remain in this flight pattern?

The names *Askelon* and *Eshkalonites* mean "migration, taken, the fire of shame; contempt." This unclean spirit is a generational assignment of shame and contempt. It migrates from one family member to another. It can take back what belongs to us; it steals our godly inheritance.

Have you found yourself gaining ground only to lose it? Has this happened often? Are you learning from the past? Are you becoming more aware of the seductions of the evil one?

If you are not careful, shame can confine you in a holding pattern and prevent you from taking the land God promised. Shame has the power to reclaim what you have possessed. Don't allow shame to overpower you. In God there are no failures; simply learn to fail "forward" and try again. Negate the stronghold of these Philistine spirits and move forward into your promise.

The Lord of the Ekronites

This king lived in Ekron, another territory allotted to Judah but regained by the Philistines. Ekron remained an enemy to the Israelites.

Both *Ekron* and *Ekronites* translate as "uprooting" and "emigration." Both of these meanings had direct bearing on the destiny of Samson, and they still seek to affect our destinies today.

First, Samson was uprooted from his destiny and purpose. Similarly, the enemy today desires to uproot us from our destinies and purposes. A constant uprooting causes God's children never to be planted firmly so that they mature.

Second, the enemy caused Samson to emigrate from his destiny. Emigration involves crossing over borders and boundaries. A devout Nazirite, there were boundaries Samson was never to cross. But he was seduced by Delilah to emigrate—to cross over borders and boundaries that took him out of his destiny and fulfillment.

In the same way, Satan tries to seduce us to emigrate from our destinies. Emigration implies moving from a homeland to foreign soil, which could be dangerous for a believer. Seduction is a boundary that none of us must cross if we desire to stay firmly planted in our destiny and fulfillment. Foreigners are considered strangers to God and are not allowed upon His holy hill of Zion (see Joel 3:17). The spirit of Delilah seduces us to cross boundaries that are not ordained by God.

Ekron also was doomed by the prophets (see Jeremiah 25:20; Amos 1:8). Do you see another pattern? The prophets are speaking into the strongholds over the Philistine cities because they are cities controlled by the devil. Prophetically, anyone who sells out to an unclean Philistine stronghold could become doomed, meaning that he or she has little hope for a promising future.

The Lord of the Gittites

The fifth king was from Gath. Goliath, the giant whom David defeated, was from the same city, so we can deduce that this king was also a behemoth! And like Goliath, who defied God, this king was probably overbearing and obnoxious, and his words were most likely intimidating. He would have towered over "Delicate Delilah" with his intimidating countenance.

Like Goliath and the king of Gath, this spirit will falsely prophesy against you and tell you that you will never be able to defeat the giant that stands in your way. Don't listen to the lies of the Philistines or allow the words of Delilah to wear you down. Our God is greater than any giant, and as He proved it to David, He will prove it to us!

Both *Gath* and *Gittite* translate as "winepress." Are you familiar with a winepress? It is a sunken area into which a grape harvest is thrown and then trodden with bare feet. The grapes are pressed so that every possible ounce of juice is extracted. Lamentations 1:15 describes the grape-treading as a metaphor for ruthless trampling and invading armies.

In the same way, Delilah applied pressure against Samson daily—to the point "that his soul was vexed unto death":

"And it came to pass, when she *pressed him daily* with her words, and urged him, so that his soul was vexed unto death" (Judges 16:16, KJV, emphasis mine). Delilah was from the city of Sorek, a name that means "choice wines." She was a vine that could intoxicate Samson with her "female pressure" to get what she wanted.

Interestingly, another translation for *Sorek* is "hiss"—a warning signal from a snake. The snake, of course, represents Satan's beguiling, manipulating and seducing nature, which stole Adam's future. The evil seducer was at work again, this time stealing Israel's future through Delilah. Isn't it interesting that Samson, a Nazirite, was so attracted to a city known for its abundance of wine?

How many times have you felt that you were in the "press"? Quite possibly you have felt as if the vineyard owner, the Lord, was pressing you to embrace change. On the other hand, maybe you have experienced the terrorizing trampling of your enemy. Either way, the pressure of the "press" extracts the best from us.

Fellow believers, we must be careful of the daily wearing down of the enemy's words. We must not allow the words of our enemy to wear us down and vex our spirits, thus allowing an entrance of death. Remember, Delilah "pressed [Samson] daily" and wore him down (Judges 16:16). Regardless of what lies the enemy speaks, we must remain committed to the future and endure the press. We must stand firmly on our promises from the Lord, not backing away from destiny.

The only avenue to travel toward our destiny is through the press of change. Do not be afraid of change. Do you remember the woman who suffered for twelve years with an issue of blood? She had to press in to receive her miracle.

She was considered unclean and was not even allowed within the city walls, and yet she pressed past her fear to touch the hem of Jesus' garment. She had to press in to receive her miracle, and she was rewarded with her healing. Saints, press in and press through any pressure the enemy hurls in your direction, and you will receive your miracle.

Dear ones, it is possible to defeat the giants who await us. Though Goliath may raise his head and falsely prophesy against us, God has said that He goes before us to defeat our enemies. Hallelujah!

Watch Out for Delilah!

The strategies that the enemy used against Samson are the same maneuvers he uses against the Body of Christ today. Satan seeks to lock us down and imprison us. He entices us with money or power. Then he targets our strengths and makes them our weaknesses. He strategizes and plans our destruction. Once we are weakened, he binds us, afflicts us and attempts to become master over us.

We need to be on high alert for Delilah. For years the Church has focused on Jezebel, but Delilah is just as seductive and evil in her own way. Though her tactics are not as blatant as Jezebel's and Athaliah's, she is nevertheless seductive and is used by the enemy to destroy destiny and purpose.

In order to be on the offense, note these characteristics of Delilah and how they differ from Jezebel and Athaliah:

- Delilah operated in a "slow seduction." Both Jezebel and Athaliah were straight and to the point, not hesitating to control and manipulate.

158

- Delilah was not power hungry, as Jezebel and Athaliah were, except for the power that mammon provides.

- Delilah was a team player (with the five Philistine kings), whereas Jezebel and Athaliah were both non-cohabitative and demanded to be in total control as individuals.

- Delilah was not a blatant murderer as Jezebel and Athaliah were. Jezebel murdered the prophets and then threatened to kill Elijah. Her daughter, Athaliah, murdered her male descendants to secure the throne of Judah. Delilah did not murder; however, she plotted and schemed against Samson in order to rob him of his life and destiny.

- Delilah was an idol worshiper, just as Jezebel and Athaliah were. But there is no indication that she brought her idols into another country, nor did she seek to influence others to worship her gods. She just seemed to look out for number one—herself!

The Number One Assignment of Delilah

The main assignment of the Delilah spirit is to attack those who have made a firm vow to the Lord. Samson forsook his Nazirite vow and lost his strength and destiny. Have you made a vow to the Lord only to be seduced later by the enemy, thus voiding your commitment?

I personally have struggled through seasons when the enemy tries desperately to uproot me from my destiny. When I am struggling emotionally, the enemy attacks relentlessly and attempts to convince me that I "do not belong" or "do not fit." Then he attempts to disconnect me from my destiny links and covenant relationships. Many times the press has been almost more than I felt I could bear, and I came close to running away from the vows I had made to serve the Lord with all my heart and might. Thank the Lord I recognized the demonic assignment desiring to steal my commitment and strength, and I was able to repent and return to Him.

Have you made a specific vow to the Lord and not fulfilled it? I encourage you to take some time and repent of any lies of the enemy that you have embraced or received. Repent of believing seducing spirits and of agreeing with the enemy's plans for your destruction. Ask the Lord to strengthen you so that you are empowered to fulfill your vows to Him. Write down some of the vows you have made, and then pray over each one. God is faithful, and He will supply the strength and determination needed to fulfill every promise.

> You will make your prayer to Him, He will hear you, and you will pay your vows. You will also declare a thing, and it will be established for you; so light will shine on your ways.
>
> Job 22:27–28

Your Hair Will Grow Again!

Samson was blinded, debased and imprisoned. It appeared that God had forsaken Samson due to his rebellion. It seemed as if Samson had suffered the worst defeat . . . and yet his hair began to grow again. And once his hair grew back, his strength returned.

The lords of the Philistines were gathering in the temple to offer sacrifices to Dagon, a god connected to Baal. (Again, we will discuss Dagon in the next chapter.) Because the Philistines were only a few miles from Zidon, the city where Jezebel was born, Baal worship was prevalent. The temple was full. The Philistines looked upon Samson, who had been summoned to perform for them. Mocking him, they made a show of his lack of power.

But Samson had a different performance in mind. He cried out to God to empower him just one last time to defeat the Philistines, the enemies of God's people. He asked to be placed between the pillars of the temple. He clutched the two middle pillars that supported the temple and pushed with all his might. The temple crumbled into pieces and fell upon the lords and all the others who were in it. He literally brought down the house, killing three thousand Philistines and destroying the idol of Dagon! Samson—and God—had the last word, for in his death he destroyed not only the Philistine kings but also more of his enemies than he had killed during his entire lifetime. Did you get that? Samson killed more Philistines after he sinned than before!

Samson could have focused on his past failures, but instead he cried out for vengeance. Rather than having a pity party for allowing himself to be enticed into sin and captivity, Samson asked for strength just one more time to defeat his enemies.

Dear ones, the Lord is on our side. Even if we have failed in the past, God promises to strengthen us. He is the God of second chances! He has great hope for our futures. He promises that if we repent of our sin, He is faithful and just to forgive us. When we feel we have forsaken our sonship, His mercy kicks in and we are forgiven of the past. Isn't our God faithful?

Precious saints of God, if you have felt as if the seduction of Delilah has stolen your strength and destiny, know this one thing: Your hair will grow again. God will give you divine strategy to defeat your enemy! Whatever has been lost in the process, God has promised to restore it (see Judges 16:28–30).

A Prayer to Defeat Delilah

Has the spirit of Delilah robbed you of your strength and determination? Do you feel that you have been seduced by the enemy to settle for less than God has for you? Maybe you feel as if you have lost your authority and sold out—as Samson did—to the enemy in some area of your life. Maybe you made a vow to the Lord and feel you cannot fulfill what you promised. The Lord is quick to forgive if we repent. Let's pray a prayer and ask the Lord to restore all that was stolen:

Father God, I praise You for who You are! You are mighty and victorious over all my enemies. Your eyes see all the injustice I have suffered at the hands of Delilah. I ask Your forgiveness for agreeing with any Philistine stronghold. In each area where the enemy has built a fortress, I ask that You tear down every stronghold with Your divine power. In areas where I have allowed the seducing spirit of Delilah to influence my thoughts or actions, I ask You to forgive me. I dethrone Satan's power over me by choosing to follow You fully and obey Your commands. I repent of other areas in my life where I have come into agreement with Satan's seductions. [Now is the time to look over this chapter where you have underlined, marked or highlighted any area in

162

which the Holy Spirit has quickened you. Take some time to repent for each one, then continue the prayer. This will kick the devil out of your life!]

Lord, empower me with Your divine strength and restore to me the joy of my salvation. I realize that You alone are my strength. There is no one like You, Lord. I now take the keys of the Kingdom and unlock the doors to financial freedom, deliverance, breakthrough [list other areas that come to your heart and mind]. With those keys I also lock out every seducing spirit and every evil assignment [list specific strongholds from which you need deliverance] in every area of my life that is unpleasing to You. I repent of unfulfilled vows, and I declare today that I am becoming empowered to fulfill Your will for my life. Thank You that I am set free because of the blood of Christ that was shed on my behalf. I thank You that as You did for Samson, You will also do for me. I shall recover all!

In Jesus' mighty name, Amen.

Be encouraged, dear ones! Just like Samson, your hair will grow again. You can rise up and defeat your enemies today!

For I know the thoughts that I think toward you, says the LORD, thoughts of peace and not of evil, to give you a future and a hope. Then you will call upon Me and go and pray to Me, and I will listen to you.

Jeremiah 29:11–12

8

PRAYING AGAINST DELILAH AND DAGON

"You will pray to him, and he will hear you, and you will fulfill your vows."

Job 22:27, NIV

Theologians debate whether Delilah was an Israelite who lived in Philistia or was actually a Philistine. Either way, she definitely had a Philistine's heart and was used by the enemy to bring down Samson. And she was operating in complete agreement with the evil influence of the Philistine god Dagon.

Once again, studying the idols to whom one submits gives insight into behavior and lifestyles. When Delilah submitted to the evil plots of the Philistines, she came into agreement with the evil deity and spirit behind their gods, Dagon and

Baal. I have gone into great detail regarding the idol Baal, the main god of Jezebel and Athaliah. Now we will closely examine Dagon, the false god worshiped by the Philistines who hired Delilah. Studying Dagon gives us greater insight into the evil influence and seductions of Delilah and helps us know how to engage her in battle most effectively.

Dagon

Dagon was the highly acclaimed national deity of the Philistines. A temple for the worship of this god could be found in each city of the Philistine pentapolis. The idol of Dagon was portrayed as a human's upper torso connected to the lower half of a fish. The cultic worship of Dagon involved human sacrifice. After the Philistines captured Samson, the five kings who hired Delilah planned a great celebration. After all, capturing this enemy was a huge feat. They believed that their god, Dagon, had delivered their archenemy into their hands. They proclaimed, "Our god has delivered into our hands our enemy" (Judges 16:24). They wanted to honor and worship their god, so they called for a human sacrifice. Most likely they intended for this sacrifice to be Samson (see Judges 16:23–24)!

But there is only one true God, and there is none like Him! Dagon was no match for Yahweh. As I stated earlier, Samson and the Lord had the final say.

Dethroning the Head and the Hands

The Israelites were challenged numerous times by the Philistines and their faith in Dagon. When Samuel was judge of Israel, the Philistines seized the Ark of God and placed it in Dagon's temple. They set the Ark close by the idol of Dagon. When the Philistines arose the next morning, Dagon had fallen on his face to the earth before the Ark of the Lord. They "resurrected" their false god by standing him up and repositioning him in his "high place." When they arose the next day, he had fallen on his face again, but this second dethroning was different from the first. This time Dagon was not just on his face; his head was detached and both palms were broken off and lay on the threshold. Only Dagon's torso was left. The false god had been dethroned by the presence of the Lord (represented by the Ark). Dagon had to bow down.

It amazes me that the Philistines did not chuck Dagon and try to keep the Ark! Oh, I know they were struck with hemorrhoids and could not wait to give the Ark back to the Israelites. But their refusal to turn from Dagon and worship instead the one true God shows how deceiving and blinding Satan can be.

Jezebel met a fate similar to that of Dagon. When Jehu had her thrown from her window, her blood was sprinkled on the wall and the horses below. Then the wild dogs devoured her body, and at her burial only her skull, feet and the palms of her hands remained (see 2 Kings 9:33–35). Jezebel's destruction had been prophesied in exactly this way.

But what was the purpose of Jezebel's skull, feet and palms being left? And why were the head and palms of Dagon severed from the rest of the idol's body? I believe these occurrences carry great significance.

First, the head represents authority and headship. When Dagon's head was severed, God was making it clear that the

167

idol had absolutely no authority. God was saying, "I am in control here." He was demonstrating in no uncertain terms that He was omnipotent.

God's presence dethrones everything that defiles His atmosphere. His presence radiates His glory, and no flesh—nor idols made from flesh—will glory (exalt itself) in His presence (see 1 Corinthians 1:29). The presence of the Lord will always declare His glory and His marvelous works. He is to be feared above all gods.

> Sing to the LORD. . . . Declare His glory. . . . He is also to be feared above all gods. For all the gods of the peoples are idols, but the LORD made the heavens. . . . Give to the LORD the glory due His name; bring an offering, and come before Him. . . . Worship the LORD in the beauty of holiness!
>
> 1 Chronicles 16:23–26, 29

The Philistines built an idol of their harvest god, trying to ensure that they would have continually fruitful harvests. Desiring to control their future, they built something with their own hands.

Man always builds structures in an attempt to get what he desires. This is why he builds idols. When we begin to build works with our own hands that are not ordained by God, we dig a deep grave. Dead works only result in death. Life comes only from the Lord.

The head also represents the intellect. As I stated before, religion promotes intellect above relationship. By removing the head of the idol, God was stating that the Philistines' religion, which was based upon their head knowledge and no relationship with the only true God, was being dethroned.

Religion precludes the need for a personal relationship with Christ. Head knowledge limits us if we do not apply knowledge with the demonstration of the Holy Spirit. I have heard it said that the greatest distance in the world is twelve inches—the distance between our hearts and our heads. Head knowledge is simply a "natural" understanding. God is Spirit and Truth. Truth can be understood with our minds, but for us to be changed into His image, He must dwell in our hearts. We cannot trust our thoughts unless our minds have been renewed through a heart relationship with our Lord.

When the dogs left the skull of Jezebel, God was declaring the same thing. He was showing that He had dethroned her illegitimate authority. All that remained was bone, signifying that "no flesh should glory in His presence" (1 Corinthians 1:29). In addition, Jezebel's painted face was gone, representing that her evil seduction had ceased.

Second, the palms of the hands represent worship, praise, power and a bowing down. In Daniel 10, the prophet had a vision of the Lord. While he was in the presence of the Lord, a hand touched him and Daniel was "set . . . upon [his] knees and upon the palms of [his] hands" (Daniel 10:10, KJV). Daniel was already on his face in the Lord's presence. He then trembled on his knees and hands, for he was already bowing to the Lord in that position. When God's presence manifests, we have to bow down because of His awesome glory and holiness.

Satan also must bow to God. "For it is written: 'As I live, says the LORD, every knee shall bow to Me, and every tongue shall confess to God'" (Romans 14:11). All powers of the occult and devil worship are dethroned in the presence of the Lord. Both Dagon and Jezebel came to their knees and hands, falling down in the presence of the Lord.

As Jezebel was being thrown down, she most likely attempted to brace herself with her hands—one last-ditch effort to control her destiny. In the end she lost all control and was forced to bow down to Elijah's declarations that "the dogs shall eat Jezebel by the wall of Jezreel" (1 Kings 21:23).

Showdowns between Yahweh and Dagon will always have the same ending: Yahweh will be victorious every time. We should never allow ourselves, however, to be seduced in the first place—as Samson was. We must guard our hearts and actions so that we are not easily influenced by Satan's evil powers.

Saul Lost His Head, Too!

How did an anointed man of God like Samson ever get to the place where he was willing to forsake his vow? Satan took the godly desire that Samson had for women and perverted it into a lust for the wrong women. He seduced Samson into straying from his destiny. We need to become more educated as to how God's children are seduced into worldly lifestyles.

Let's take a look at another anointed man of God, Saul, who was seduced by the Philistine spirit. King Saul lost his life during a battle with the Philistines. Actually, he took his own life. After Saul's death the Philistines beheaded him and then stole his armor and placed it in the temple of their gods. Then they hung his head in the temple of Dagon!

How could this have happened? How could the Philistines ever have taken the head of God's anointed and placed it in the same temple as their idol? You may remember that Saul had lost favor with God. The once-chosen, anointed leader of Israel had decided to disobey God. God had told Saul to utterly destroy all the Amalekites, but instead he chose to preserve their king, Agag. Samuel, the prophet, rebuked Saul for this action and proclaimed that God had rejected him as king. Samuel stated that Saul's rebellion was "as the sin of witchcraft, and stubbornness . . . as iniquity and idolatry" (1 Samuel 15:23, KJV). The Lord had judged Saul's heart and actions and compared his rebellion to witchcraft and his stubbornness to worshiping idols.

Witchcraft is any attempt to control the future, and this is a form of idolatry because it involves seeking another source over God. God compared it to consulting a soothsayer for direction, which is similar to creating and worshiping idols with the purpose of expecting them to "perform" for us. Saul's disobedience stripped him of God's protection, spiritual armor and favor, and he subsequently died in battle.

If only Saul could have "kept his head" during battle! Maybe then he would not have fallen to the Philistines and literally lost his head.

When the Philistines found Saul's dead body, they took his armor and his head, and there is significance to each of these. Dagon was the principal god of the Philistines who ruled over the other false gods. He was the "grain god," the god of the harvest. But the Philistines also worshiped Ashtoreth, the goddess of war and fertility. Supposedly

171

these two false gods were "married," and worshiping them together represented an ultimate victory over their foes. Taking Saul's armor and placing it in one of their temples (most likely that of Ashtoreth) signified that the Israelites had no defense against the Philistine god Ashtoreth. Taking the head of Saul to Dagon's temple made the statement that the headship of Israel had bowed to their god. In the place where Dagon's head had fallen before the Ark, Saul's head now bowed to Dagon.

Taking Saul's head and placing it in the temple of Dagon was a deliberate act, an in-your-face action against the almighty God. It was as if the devil were saying, "I will seduce and distort man's mind and cause him to believe me over God. I will turn him against God!" Satan desires to seduce and defile our minds (heads) concerning the truth. If he can control our minds, he can win the battle.

Satan has tried to distort our minds for centuries by attempting to negate the power of the Holy Spirit. He has convinced us that studying the Scriptures is the only thing necessary to be a Christian. Though we obviously need the Scriptures, we also need the Holy Spirit to empower us to properly interpret and apply the Word. Jesus taught the Scriptures *and* demonstrated its truths. We must do the same.

How to Pray against Dagon's Evil Influence

The Lord has given us prayer strategies to defeat Dagon's influence. Let's examine these strategies.

First, it is important to recognize that because Delilah was employed by the Philistines, who worshiped Dagon, she

172

had come into agreement with both parties—the Philistines and the idol. To defeat the seducing spirit that influenced Delilah, we must target our prayers against the evil forces behind Dagon and break ties to any lies and deceptions with which we have agreed. The devil has no power unless we agree with him.

Second, remember that Dagon was worshiped for harvest, fruitfulness and power. Spiritually, this translates into provision, the spirit of mammon, reproduction and power over enemies. In order to defeat Dagon, then, we should direct our prayers toward overthrowing the powers of darkness that cause poverty and lack of fruitfulness. We also should take authority over every barren situation. David addressed Goliath as an uncircumcised Philistine. Having our hearts circumcised to receive the Word and Truth of God therefore empowers us to stand against our enemies. It also prevents us from being "stiff-necked" and keeps us free from any Philistine influence or idolatry. "Therefore circumcise the foreskin of your heart, and be stiff-necked no longer" (Deuteronomy 10:16).

Third, we must not allow the devil to get a-"head," like he did when he took Saul's. Most of the battles we fight are between our ears. Head knowledge, or mindsets, can interfere with receiving present truth and can hinder one's faith in God's ability to perform the supernatural. We must therefore renew our minds with truth. Renewing our minds does not just affect our minds; it totally changes us. It causes every part of us to be transformed into His image. Through the process of transformation, each of us presents his or her body as "a living sacrifice, holy, acceptable to God" (Romans 12:1). Through transformation we are empowered to no longer be "conformed to this world" but equipped to "prove what is that good and acceptable and perfect will of God" (Romans 12:2). How awesome! We get a new heart and a new life when our minds become renewed. There is no place for idolatry if we renew our minds to the truths of God.

Fourth, we must put on the armor of God every day. God takes excellent care of His soldiers by giving them His name, His authority, His Word and His armor. Both precious and priceless, the armor of God protects us from the fiery darts of every seducing spirit. In the same way that the Philistines took Saul's armor, Satan would love to take ours, because if he can steal our armor, then he can seduce us. And keep in mind that it is the armor "of God"—His very own armor!—that He gives to each of us to wear during battle.

Let's take a more in-depth look at the armor of God.

The Armor of God

Clothing ourselves with God's armor prepares us to withstand any attack from the devil. It empowers us to defeat every seducing spirit that attempts to yoke us with the past.

Finally, my brethren, be strong in the Lord and in the power of His might. Put on the whole armor of God, that you may be able to stand against the wiles of the devil. For we do not wrestle against flesh and blood, but against principalities, against powers, against the rulers of the darkness of this age, against spiritual hosts of wickedness in the heavenly places. Therefore take up the whole armor of God, that you may be able to withstand in the evil day, and having done all, to stand.

Stand therefore, having girded your waist with truth, having put on the breastplate of righteousness, and having shod your feet with the preparation of the gospel of peace; above all, taking the shield of faith with which you will be able to quench all the fiery darts of the wicked one. And take the helmet of salvation, and the sword of the Spirit, which is the word of God.

Ephesians 6:10–17

The Girdle, or Belt, of Truth is important because a belt holds the rest of the armor in place. The belt represents a clear understanding of God's Word. Without truth, light cannot penetrate darkness. Jesus is the Truth and also the Light. He is the substance that holds the rest of our armor together. When we have Jesus, all darkness from the enemy has to disperse. When exposed to the Truth and the Light, every occult spirit that tries to remain hidden has to flee. To battle an occult stronghold, therefore, we must be daily equipped with our girdle.

The Breastplate of Righteousness is the most important part of our armor. Jesus is our righteousness, and we put Him on first. Knowing that there is not one thing in us that makes us righteous keeps us humble and "bowed down" to His greatness and glory. And recognizing that we have life only because of what Christ did for us on the cross prevents us from giving any place to pride or idolatry. The breastplate protects our heart. David said, "Your word I have hidden in my heart, that I might not sin against You" (Psalm 119:11). Our passion for the Lord is protected if we daily apply the breastplate.

The Gospel of Peace gives protection to our feet. The Lord told His children that everywhere the soles of their feet tread lay the promise of victory (see Deuteronomy 11:24). It is the same for us today. But why does the armor of God involve our feet walking in peace?

One of my favorite Scripture passages is when Jesus fell asleep right in the middle of a life-threatening storm (see Matthew 8:23–27; Mark 4:35–41; Luke 8:22–25). The disciples were terrified and awakened Jesus for help. With authority, Jesus rebuked the wind and said, "Peace, be still!" (Mark 4:39). Jesus walked in peace, and it was that same peace that stilled the storm. In Bill Johnson's book, *When Heaven Invades Earth*, the author summed up this passage perfectly: "You have authority only over the storm you can sleep in." After stilling the storm, Jesus went on to address the disciples' unbelief, and this applies to us, as well. If we are not able to trust Him and believe that He is able to take care of even the little sparrows, then we allow ourselves to be robbed of His peace. When we doubt Him, in whom are we putting our trust? Idolatry is putting our trust in anything other than our Lord. Winning the battle requires walking in peace and complete trust in our God.

The Shield of Faith provides protection for the entire body. With this shield, we are able to quench every fiery dart of the enemy. The Scripture states that God is our shield and our fortress (see Psalm 18:2; 144:2). The Lord told Abraham, "I am thy shield, and thy exceeding great reward" (Genesis 15:1, KJV). The Lord is well able to protect and shield us from our enemies. No idol or false belief will stand in the presence of our God.

The Helmet of Salvation protects the soldier's head. Let's determine not to be like King Saul and fall prey to the Philistines. By keeping our heads on straight, we will not be confronted with the sin of idolatry. Protecting our heads protects our mindsets and allows us to renew our minds with God's truth.

In addition, our hope of deliverance from sin lies in our salvation. The word *salvation* means much more than being saved from eternal damnation. The Greek word for *salvation* is fully translated as "deliverance, preservation and safety," and it involves being whole and complete in Christ. The word also translates as "deliverance from the molestation of enemies." Molestation is not limited to a sexual context; it refers to crossing a physical boundary. The enemy wants to trespass on God's property. So wearing the helmet of salvation prevents the evil one from crossing boundaries in our lives. If he has lied to you concerning God's promise, for example, then he is trespassing because God has already declared that you are the apple of His eye and His love toward you is everlasting.

The Sword of the Spirit is our offensive weapon. All other parts of the armor defend, but the sword positions us to move forward. The sword of the Spirit is the Word of God. It is alive and full of power. Whenever we speak God's Word, it goes forth and accomplishes what God intends: "For the word of God is living and powerful, and sharper than any two-edged sword" (Hebrews 4:12). Using the sword of the Spirit releases life into dead situations. It demolishes death structures of idolatry and destroys the threefold cord that threatens the future. Psalm 129:4 states, "The LORD is righteous; He has cut in pieces the cords of

177

the wicked." Our sword is sharper than any curse. It cuts away premature death, cancer, infirmity and generational curses. God's Word always releases increase (see Acts 12:24). If we desire fruitfulness and increase, then we need only to speak God's Word into the desired circumstances. The Philistines built Dagon because they needed an increased harvest; we need only to worship the King of Kings and speak His Word. Hallelujah!

What Part of the Armor Do You Need?

Now I want you to take a few minutes to consider the areas where the enemy is attempting to seduce or tempt you. What armor do you need to wear to achieve victory in each area? I have provided space below for you to write each area, a Scripture you can use to overcome the temptation and the piece of armor you need for victory. Then, instead of my writing a prayer for you, I encourage you to write your own prayer of deliverance that pertains specifically to each area.

After you have completed this assignment, be sure to pray daily for the power to resist the devil. This will empower you on a daily basis to defeat the enemy. When I am going through a daily press from the enemy, I have learned from experience to dethrone his evil words, repent for listening to him in the first place and then build an altar to God through praise.

It works! God is so good, isn't He?

Seductive plan of the devil #1:

Scripture to overcome the temptation:

The piece of God's armor I need for victory:

Prayer for deliverance from the enemy:

Seductive plan of the devil #2:
  Scripture to overcome the temptation:

  The piece of God's armor I need for victory:

  Prayer for deliverance from the enemy:

Seductive plan of the devil #3:
  Scripture to overcome the temptation:

  The piece of God's armor I need for victory:

  Prayer for deliverance from the enemy:

Daily Prayer of Empowerment

Father, in the mighty name of Jesus, Your Son, I pray that You empower me to defeat my enemy. I repent of not trusting You and not walking in peace. [Now repent of any other areas of sin that come to mind and ask for forgiveness.] I ask You to empower me to renew my mind and to cleanse me and create in me a clean heart. I take authority over every seduction of Satan and his plans to destroy my life. I bind the evil works of Delilah and the Philistine stronghold. I command the doors that have been opened to Satan's seductions to become closed and locked. I dethrone Satan from his seated position in my life and circumstances. I ask that You empower me to fulfill every vow and commitment I have made to serve You. I desire to be a pure vessel, fit for the Master's use. Today I choose to fight for my inheritance. I will not be like Esau and sell my birthright for a bowl of soup or fleshly desire. I will cherish my inheritance and become determined to possess all that You have promised to me.

In Jesus' name, Amen.

CONCLUSION

See and Believe!

This book has been an intense journey. It has exposed the lies of the enemy and how he works through the seductive spirits of Jezebel, Athaliah and Delilah, three very strong satanic influences targeting the Body of Christ.

Exposure means that something is exposed and, therefore, we are able to *see* it. Through the exposure of this threefold influence, we *see* the destructive plans of Satan and know how to thwart them. Without exposure we easily lose vision—especially when the primary reason for the attack is to abort destiny through loss of vision. Unless we clearly see God's plans for our lives and the pathways to fulfill vision, we have little hope for the future. The Word says that without vision we will perish, and if we see no escape from the clutches of the enemy, then defeat lies around the nearest corner. When sight is restored, however, and we are empowered to see our future, we can run full throttle toward the finish line.

In Jeremiah 1:11, God asked the prophet what he saw. Jeremiah responded by saying that he saw a branch of an almond tree budding. The Lord said, "You have seen correctly, for I am watching to see that my word is fulfilled" (verse 12, NIV). The first tree to bud in a new season is the almond tree. God was revealing to Jeremiah that a new season was coming forth, and He was promising to bring forth what Jeremiah had seen. God had lifted the veil from this prophet's eyes to see into the future.

Dear ones, allow me to ask you the same question: What do you see? I encourage you to ask the Lord to remove the veil of despair and allow you to see a new season before you. It is your time of breakthrough. It is a time of great anticipation. And if you will press in to God's promise, He is promising to fulfill what He has spoken.

Will You Tolerate Satan's Threefold Cord?

During the writing and editing of this book, I have had several dreams concerning the demonic powers of Jezebel, Athaliah and Delilah. In each dream the Lord spoke clearly and told me I was tolerating the Jezebel principality in my life through levels of compromise. Then He said that the other two strongholds, Athaliah and Delilah, gained entrance because I had first tolerated Jezebel, and now I was being seduced to tolerate the other two evil influences, as well. I ran once again to pick up the closest Webster's to reexamine the word *tolerate*. I was immediately convicted to repent.

To *tolerate* involves allowing something in our lives that is not "wholly approved." This spoke loudly to me! Who is not approving? It is the Lord Himself, of course, who does not approve of Jezebel or her actions. The conviction I felt was not coming from my own mind but from my heart because Jesus lives in me, and His Holy Spirit convicts us of sin. The Lord has made a tabernacle in my heart, and if I am tolerating Jezebel, He is displeased with me.

Remember that Jesus condemned the church of Thyatira for tolerating Jezebel (see Revelation 2:18–23). He was telling the people that they tolerated her because He was not dwelling in their hearts and that they had allowed themselves to be seduced by her evil influence. Christ also addressed her seed, Athaliah, condemning her to death (see Revelation 2:23). Though Christ did not directly address the stronghold of Delilah, He specifically addressed the seduction of the enemy as He addressed the stronghold of Jezebel.

Weigh the Facts

All too often we make choices without fully examining the facts. God is calling us to *deliberation*, a weighing of the facts. Considering the factual evidence you have "seen" in this book concerning three very strong seductive forces, have you fully decided that you can no longer tolerate Jezebel and her cohorts?

For years the enemy has targeted our generations, seduced the priesthood and murdered unborn children. He has schemed with "deliberate" intent to destroy each of our destinies and to rob us of our inheritance. How many of us are living the fulfilled lives promised to us? If by reading this book you have deliberated—weighed the facts—and realized how much more life and breakthrough God has for you to experience, then it is truly time to take immediate action. Repentance always puts us in right standing with the Father. He desires to set us free and empower us to experience life to its fullest.

Believe

In 2 Kings 6:24–33 we read that Israel was under siege by its enemies. There was a great famine in the land and no food in storage. The women in the city became so hungry that they murdered their own children and ate them. How could God's people become cannibals? I pondered this passage for days seeking revelation. As a minister who travels extensively, I have seen that when spiritually dry and thirsty, many Christians turn on each other rather than focus on the real enemy. And at times we "eat our own seed," meaning that we do not believe what God has placed inside us, such as a prophetic word or a prophetic teaching concerning breakthrough. In essence, we devour the seed that He has declared. We become "Christian cannibals."

The story goes on to say that when the king of Israel realized the women were devouring their seed, he grew angry with the prophet! Rather than repenting of any open doors that might have allowed the siege, he immediately blamed Elisha. All too often we choose not to examine our own sin or lack of relationship with God when we do not experience breakthrough.

Elisha came on the scene and declared that Israel soon would experience a breakthrough (see 2 Kings 7). He prophesied that there would be an abundant food supply within 24 hours. The king's right-hand man, a man of great authority, stated his opinion that even if the windows of heaven were to open this could not happen. The prophet then declared, "It will happen. Others will partake of it, and you will see it, but not eat of it!" (verse 19, paraphrased). Amazingly, it happened! Four lepers who had been placed outside the city walls decided to take a risk. Rather than die where they were, they risked their lives to go to the camp of their enemies to find food. As they approached the enemy camp, God magnified their footsteps and made it sound like an invading army. The enemies were so fearful that they all fled, leaving their food supplies, horses and tents—major spoils of war! When the king of Israel discovered that food was available, he had the doubting scoffer, his right-hand man, open the gates of the city. This man was subsequently trampled to death by the people running to partake of the spoils. Friends, one must pay a high price for doubt and unbelief.

Are you ready to believe? Will you believe that God has a Promised Land for you? Have you pressed beyond doubt and unbelief, and are you now empowered to take the spoils of war?

"It is not over until the fat lady sings!" When I was a child I did not understand this phrase. Recently I watched an old movie—you know, a prehistoric film clip—in which a really overweight woman sang at the end of the show. That was the sign that the show was over. Precious ones, the show is not over! Although the enemy may appear to have had the upper hand, he has not defeated us! The showdown is just beginning as we rise up and fight the good fight of faith. And defeating our enemy begins with our belief.

God says that all things are possible if we believe (see Mark 9:23). Are you ready for the possible? I am! Why don't you come with me to that land today?

Be on the lookout for your breakthrough. Joy comes in the morning!

Expect the supernatural to invade the natural.

Live each day with great expectation. God wants to perform for you today.

Intercede for your family and your nation, and expect God to intervene.

Excel in your expectations of God as you move from faith to faith, glory to glory and strength to strength.

Victory is yours as you gain hope for your future.

Excitement is contagious! Share the revelation you have gained with someone else.

BELIEVE with him or her for a mighty move of God's Spirit!

NOTES

1. W. E. Vine, Merrill F. Unger, and William White Jr., *Vine's Complete Expository Dictionary of Old and New Testament Words* (Nashville: Thomas Nelson, 1997).

2. Sandie Freed, *Dream On: Unlocking Your Dreams and Visions* (Hurst, Tex.: Zion Ministries, 2005), 141.

3. John Paul Jackson, *Unmasking the Jezebel Spirit* (North Sutton, N.H.: Streams Publications, 2002), 68.

4. These names are a result of my own personal research and also are noted in Jonas Clark, *Jezebel: Seducing Goddess of War* (Hallandale Beach, Fla.: Spirit of Life Publishing, 1998), 59–60.

5. Sandie Freed, *Strategies from Heaven's Throne: Claiming the Life God Wants for You* (Grand Rapids: Chosen, 2007), 36–39.

RECOMMENDED READING

Clark, Jonas. *Jezebel, Seducing Goddess of War*. Hallandale, Fla.: Spirit of Life Publishing, 2002.

Freed, Sandie. *Destiny Thieves: Defeat Seducing Spirits and Achieve Your Purpose in God*. Grand Rapids: Chosen Books, 2006.

Freed, Sandie. *Dream On: Unlocking Your Dreams and Visions*. Hurst, Tex.: Zion Ministries, 2005. Available from Zion Ministries: www.zionministries.us.

Freed, Sandie. *Strategies from Heaven's Throne: Claiming the Life God Wants for You*. Grand Rapids: Chosen Books, 2007.

Greenwald, Gary. *Seductions Exposed: The Spiritual Dynamics of Relationships*. New Kensington, Penn.: Whitaker House, 2003.

Hamon, Bill. *Prophets, Pitfalls and Principles: God's Prophetic People Today*. Shippensburg, Penn.: Destiny Image, 1991.

Jackson, John Paul. *Unmasking the Jezebel Spirit*. North Sutton, N.H.: Streams Publications, 2002.

Johnson, Bill. *When Heaven Invades Earth: A Practical Guide to a Life of Miracles*. Shippensburg, Penn.: Treasure House, 2003.

Pierce, Chuck D., and Rebecca Wagner Sytsema. *The Future War of the Church: How We Can Defeat Lawlessness and Bring God's Order to the Earth*. Ventura, Calif.: Renew Books, 2001.

Robeson, Carol and Jerry. *Strongman's His Name . . . What's His Game?: An Authoritative Biblical Approach to Spiritual Warfare*. Woodburn, Ore.: Shiloh Publishing House, 1983.

Stevens, Dr. Selwyn. *Unmasking Freemasonry: Removing the Hoodwink*. www.jubilee-resources.com. .

Varner, Kelley. *The More Excellent Ministry*. Shippensburg, Penn.: Destiny Image Publishers, 1988.

Wagner, Doris M. *How to Minister Freedom: Helping Others Break the Bonds of Sexual Brokenness, Emotional Woundedness, Demonic Oppression and Occult Bondage*. Ventura, Calif.: Regal Books, 2005.

Wentroble, Barbara. *Prophetic Intercession: Unlocking Miracles and Releasing the Blessings of God*. Ventura, Calif.: Gospel Light Worldwide, 1993.

Yoder, Barbara. *The Breaker Anointing*. Colorado Springs: Wagner Publications, 2001.

Author's Note: Many excellent sources expose the occult involvement of Freemasonry. In addition, many quality ministers can walk others through deliverance from the spirits connected with this false religion. Among other organizations, Zion Ministries offers deliverance sessions. If you are interested, contact our website: www.zionministries.us.

Sandie Freed and her husband, Mickey, are the founders and directors of Zion Ministries in Bedford, Texas. Together they pastored a local church in Texas for more than fourteen years, and today they apostolically oversee the Zion Kingdom Training Center, which trains and activates the Body of Christ in spiritual gifting.

Sandie is an ordained prophetess with Christian International Ministries and travels extensively, teaching prophetic truths to the Body of Christ. Sandie and Mickey also travel nationally and internationally as the Christian International IMPACT Team, in which they apostolically and prophetically oversee regions and churches.

Sandie has written three books: *Destiny Thieves: Defeat Seducing Spirits and Achieve Your Purpose in God; Strategies from Heaven's Throne: Claiming the Life God Wants for You;* and *Dream On: Unlocking Your Dreams and Visions.* She has a master's degree in biblical theology and is often a featured guest on television and radio, where she has shared her testimony of God's healing and delivering power. A gifted minister in dreams and visions and spiritual discernment, Sandie is a sought-after speaker and seminar instructor for her insight on dreams and visions and discerning strongholds over individuals, churches and regions. She is known for her powerful, down-to-earth messages that release life transformation and encouragement.

Sandie and Mickey have a daughter, Kim, and a son-in-law, Matt, who are active ordained ministers with Zion Ministries.

To contact Sandie Freed regarding speaking engagements, reach her at:

Zion Ministries
P.O. Box 5487
Hurst, TX 76054
(817) 589-8811 or (817) 284-5966
zionministries1@sbcglobal.net

For information on Zion Ministries' seminars, such as "The School of Prophets," "Advanced Prophetic Training" and "Prophetic Intercession Training," or to see recent teaching, books, tapes or itinerary, log on to the Zion Ministries website: www.zionministries.us.